W9-BUM-468

The
GARDENER'S
YEAR

Horticultural Consultant ❧ Veronica Peerless
Senior Editor ❧ Chauney Dunford
Project Art Editor ❧ Clare Marshall
Managing Editor ❧ Penny Warren
DK Picture Library ❧ Claire Cordier
Senior Jacket Creative ❧ Nicola Powling
Pre-production Producer ❧ Ray Williams
Senior Producer ❧ Ché Creasey
Art Director ❧ Jane Bull
Publisher ❧ Mary Ling

DK Publishing
North American Editor ❧ Kate Johnsen
Senior Editor ❧ Shannon Beatty

This edition first published in 2015 by DK Publishing, 4th floor,
345 Hudson Street, New York, New York 10014

14 15 16 17 18 19 10 9 8 7 6 5 4 3 2 1
001–184576–Sept/2015

Copyright © 2015 Dorling Kindersley Limited
A Penguin Random House Company

All rights reserved
Without limiting the rights under copyright reserved, above, no part of this publication
may be reproduced, stored in or introduced into a retrieval system, or transmitted,
in any form, or by any means (electronic, mechanical, photocopying, recording, or
otherwise), without the prior written permission of both the copyright owner and the
above publisher of this book.

Published in Great Britain by
Dorling Kindersley Limited.

A catalog record for this book is available from the Library of Congress.

ISBN 978-1-4654-2457-0

DK books are available at special discounts when purchased in bulk for sales promotions,
premiums, fund-raising, or educational use. For details, contact: DK Publishing Special Markets,
345 Hudson Street, New York, New York 10014 or SpecialSales@dk.com.

Printed and bound in China by Leo Paper Products Ltd.

A WORLD OF IDEAS:
SEE ALL THERE IS TO KNOW

www.dk.com

The GARDENER'S YEAR

CONTENTS

FOUR SEASONS

Spring

The first flowers

It's thrilling to watch the garden finally wake up after a long, cold, and in many places, sodden, winter. It starts slowly, with a few green shoots and welcome early flowers peeping through the soil, and gradually builds into a joyful crescendo of color. This is many gardeners' favorite season, ripe with fresh new growth and possibilities. It's also one of the busiest times. As the soil warms up and the days lengthen, there's the sowing, planting, pruning, and weeding to be done.

Bulbs are a vital part of the spring show, as the tiny, delicate blooms of irises and crocuses are followed by grape hyacinths, swathes of daffodils, and, finally, masses of colorful tulips.

If you have a tree that bears blossom in your garden, such as a magnolia, ornamental cherry, or crab apple, it will be the star of the show now. And some of our most spectacular shrubs, such as rhododendrons, camellias, and lilacs, put on a fantastic display in spring, too.

The earliest crops

Spring is a very busy time in the edible garden, as it's when seed sowing begins in earnest for harvests later in the year. But it's not all hard work. It's also a time to enjoy the first of your crops: tasty broad beans, the sweet spears of asparagus, and the earliest fruit crop of all, gooseberries.

You can also sow and eat speedy crops that are ready to harvest just a few weeks after sowing, such as salad leaves, baby beets, and radishes. Then, of course, there are the overwintered crops, such as crisp kale and the hearty root vegetables.

IN THE GARDEN

Summer

Flourishing blooms

Summer is all about flowers, whether in containers, hanging baskets, or borders, and it's when most gardens are at their peak. Herbaceous perennials are now in the spotlight. Elegant spires of delphiniums, fleeting Oriental poppies, glamorous peonies, and trusty hardy geraniums begin the show, followed by a riot of color from phlox, penstemons, and African lilies. These are supported by attractive annuals that were sown in spring, such as cosmos, tagetes, and zinnias. Roses of all kinds are freely blooming, as are clematis and other climbers.

Tender bedding plants, such as pelargoniums, fuchsias, and petunias come to the fore, creating eye-catching spectacles in containers, hanging baskets, and windowboxes. You can also enjoy a bounty of cut flowers for the house, with sweet peas, cornflowers, and stocks, to name but a few.

There are still jobs to do in summer, such as watering, weeding, and deadheading, but don't forget to relax and enjoy your garden.

Edible abundance

The fruits of your labors in spring are rewarded now, as you begin harvesting delicious early new potatoes and garden peas, then string and green beans, snow peas, zucchini, garlic and onions, and vibrant Swiss chard. It's also a productive time in the fruit garden, with tart gooseberries,

currants, and mountains of plump strawberries to enjoy, followed by cherries, blueberries, summer raspberries, and plums.

Fall

The fiery finale

If summer is about flowers, fall is about foliage, fruits, and berries. The leaves of many deciduous trees, climbers, and shrubs, such as maples, Boston ivy, and spindle tree, put on a fiery show before falling.
Meanwhile, shrubs, such as cotoneaster and pyracantha, are smothered in berries, while shrub roses bear an abundance of bright red hips.

There are plenty of flowers to enjoy, too. Many annuals and perennials, such as cosmos and penstemons, will power on until the first frosts. In early fall, colorful dahlias are at their peak, as are other exotic-looking plants, such as bananas, ginger lilies, and cannas. These are followed by perennial asters, in shades of white, purple, or blue, along with late-blooming nerine lilies and chrysanthemums. This is also when ornamental grasses really come into their own, as their stems and plumes turn golden, bringing texture to the border, and complementing the seedheads of perennials that are now dying back.

It's the end of the growing season, but it's also a time to look ahead, too. Fall is the time to plant new perennials, trees, and shrubs, as well as early bulbs for the spring to come.

A grand feast

Now is the time to enjoy fall's bounty of corn, tomatoes, chilies, and eggplants; the last of the zucchini and beans; along with squashes and pumpkins. And there's fruit, too, such as apples and pears, to eat now or to store for later, along with fall-fruiting raspberries that can continue cropping until the first proper frosts.

Winter

Cold comforts

Traditionally, borders were cut back or cleared in fall, leaving them bare. Now many perennials and grasses are left standing over winter, as their shapes and forms bring interest to the garden while providing food and habitat for wildlife. Winter is the season for evergreen foliage, colorful stems, and interesting bark, as well as winter-flowering shrubs, many of which have a powerful scent. There are also winter bedding plants to enjoy, especially when planted near the house where they can be seen. And just as the year starts with bulbs, so it ends that way, with aconites and snowdrops that thrive grown *en masse* beneath deciduous trees and shrubs.

Cool crops

There's a surprising amount to harvest during winter, such as parsnips, cabbages, leeks, and kale, plus Brussels sprouts for Christmas dinner. Many can be left in the garden until you need them, and often taste better having been frosted.

ABOUT THIS BOOK

Organized by season, the plants and crops included are featured in the order in which they are at their best in the garden—hence spring runs from daffodils to gooseberries. Exactly when plants and crops are at their prime, however, is affected by how and where you garden, and also your local weather conditions.

The tasks featured also appear in the order they should ideally be done, though this, too, will vary for the same reasons. As a rule, judge the growing conditions outside and garden accordingly.

KEY TO SYMBOLS
- ❦ **Plant type**
- ♠ **Height**
- ◣ **Spread**
- ☼ **Aspect**
- ⊚ **Soil type**
- ↓ **When to plant**
- ◎ **When to harvest**

Spring

Signs of Spring

Spring is one of the most exciting seasons in the garden, when all around you signs of life are poking through the soil or filling the air. It is a time of contrasts—a hint of the summer to come with the threat of winter chill still lingering.

Vernal equinox

Spring is triggered by the vernal equinox, when the tilt in the Earth's orbit means the Northern Hemisphere begins to face the Sun at a more direct angle. This increases the warming effect of the Sun on the Earth, dispelling the cold of winter.

Day length

Equinox means "equal night" and marks the point in the Earth's orbit when the Sun is above and below the horizon for an equal time—day and night are the same length. Following the vernal equinox in mid-March, daylight hours increase and nights become shorter. This is most pronounced in northern regions, where nights can be short, staying dark for just a few hours.

Weather

The weather at this time is highly variable, and even when spring has technically begun, conditions can remain wintery for several weeks. Hard frost and snow are common in early spring, which is often then replaced by persistent rain. Spring can also bring droughts, strong wind, and short-lived heat waves, creating challenging conditions for gardeners. The trick is to observe the weather where you are, check the forecasts, and to make the most of good spells.

Temperature

Although cold at first, spring brings improving conditions, with daytime temperatures rising from between 36–48°F to 43–59°F (2–9°C to 6–15°C) on average by the end of the season. This rise, combined with regular rainfall and increasing day length, is ideal for powering the rapid plant growth seen at this time, as seeds start to germinate, and trees, shrubs, bulbs, and perennials come into growth again.

Plant science

Spring may herald warmer weather, but plants only come into growth when growing conditions are ideal. To ensure this, they have evolved their own ways to tell the weather.

SEEDS

Unlike trees, shrubs, and perennials, seeds can remain dormant for years, even centuries, and will only germinate once certain factors indicating that growing conditions are suitable are met. Though it varies between plant species, this is typically a specific combination of temperature, light, moisture, and time, but can even include exposure to extreme events, such as fire or digestion by an animal. When the conditions are right, hormones in the seed trigger it into growth. If conditions suddenly change, however, such as an untimely dry or cold spell, the seed will often abort germination and die.

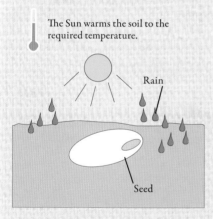

The Sun warms the soil to the required temperature.

Rain

Seed

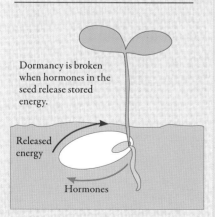

Dormancy is broken when hormones in the seed release stored energy.

Released energy

Hormones

PERENNIALS

Herbaceous perennials may appear lifeless while they are dormant but certain tissues do remain active at this time, effectively monitoring the surrounding conditions. The precise mechanism is unknown, and varies between plant species, but perennials will only emerge from dormancy when moisture, temperature, and light levels are suitable for growth. Hormones in the plant then initiate the conversion of energy-rich starch stored in the roots (as found in potatoes, for example) into sugar that is used to power the formation of new leaves and stems.

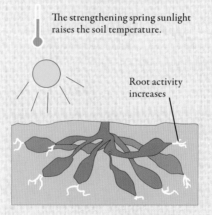

The strengthening spring sunlight raises the soil temperature.

Root activity increases

Hormones release stored energy to produce buds.

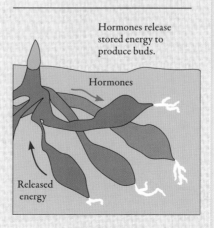

Hormones

Released energy

TREES AND SHRUBS

Trees and shrubs only emerge from dormancy once their "chilling requirement" has been met. This a period when the temperature has stayed between 34–45°F (1–7°C) for around 20 consecutive days in a row. If a warm spell occurs while the plant is dormant, its stopwatch is reset until the correct period is achieved. Temperature changes are variable, so plants also monitor the changing day length using special cells, which is a more consistent measure of the changing season. Once the chilling requirement has been met, and the days are increasing in length, plants come back into growth for another year.

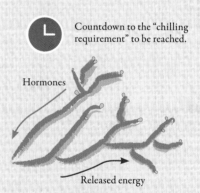

Countdown to the "chilling requirement" to be reached.

Hormones

Released energy

Energy stored in the plant is released and buds form.

The buds open into new leaves that provide energy for the plant.

Energy produced

Daffodils

The cheery trumpet blooms of daffodils, known botanically as *Narcissus*, bring swathes of color and scent to borders, lawns, and pots throughout spring, and they also make wonderful cut flowers. There are hundreds of types to grow, from miniature species to large-flowered hybrids, which vary in color from gold to white, and even pink-tinged. Many are bicolored, with their trumpets and outer ring of petals in contrasting shades.

Caring for daffodils

Daffodils are planted as dormant bulbs in early fall (*see p.258* and *p.260*), at a depth of three times the height of the bulb. For the best display, plant them in natural drifts or clumps, spaced according to the instructions on the package. Deadhead spent blooms to conserve the plant's energy and allow the foliage to gradually die off before cutting it back; removing the leaves too soon weakens the plant. Daffodils form clumps over time that can become congested. If the display deteriorates, lift and divide larger clumps during fall (*see p.261*).

> **AT A GLANCE**
> ❧ **Plant type** Hardy bulb
> ⬆ **Height** 6–20in (15–50cm)
> 🍃 **Spread** 2–4in (5–10cm)
> ☼ **Aspect** Full sun or partial shade
> ◉ **Soil type** Moist but well drained

Which to choose

The traditional image of daffodils is of the golden, large-flowered varieties, such as 'Carlton' (*right*), but there are many other types to grow.

Dwarf varieties, such as 'Jack Snipe' (*above*), have a dainty appearance and look most at home in smaller sites and in containers.

White daffodils, such as 'Toto' (*above*), offer a contrast to the familiar golden forms. For greater impact, plant a mixture of shades.

Species daffodils, such as *N. bulbocodium* (*above*), have simple charm. Most are small plants, ideal for rockeries and containers.

Narcissus 'Carlton'

Camellia x *williamsii* 'Joan Trehane'

Camellias

Shrubby camellias give a spectacular show in spring, flowering for weeks in shades of pink, white, and red. Acid-loving, these large, dense evergreens grow well in containers, so can even be enjoyed in areas with alkaline soil. New plants establish best when planted in fall, though container-grown specimens can be planted at any time so long as they are kept moist. Even though the plants are fully hardy, their flowers can be damaged if they thaw too quickly after frost, so position camellias away from direct morning sunlight. Established plants need little routine care or pruning. Simply deadhead them to keep them tidy.

AT A GLANCE
❦ **Plant type** Hardy evergreen shrub
⬧ **Height** 3–15ft (1–5m)
◣ **Spread** 3–12ft (1–4m)
☀ **Aspect** Full sun to light shade
◉ **Soil type** Acid, moist, and well drained

Choosing camellias

Spring-flowering camellias are all grown in the same way and offer a wealth
of flower types—from elegantly simple to elaborate confections—in a range of
different sizes. Height and spread varies with variety; compact camellias are
ideal for large containers but larger forms are best in borders. For year-round
interest, choose varieties with variegated foliage, such as *C. × williamsii*
'Golden Spangles'.

Camellia japonica
'Elegans Supreme'

C. japonica
'Tricolor'

C. reticulata
'Captain Rawes'

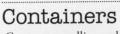

C. japonica 'Charlotte
de Rothschild'

Containers

Compact camellias, such as
C. japonica 'Guilio Nuccio'
and 'Nuccio's Gem' are ideal
for growing in containers.
Choose as large a planter as
you have space for, ensure it
has drainage holes, and fill it
with acid soil mix—essential
for acid-loving plants. Keep
camellias well watered,
especially in summer when
the new flower buds form,
and mulch with compost
each spring.

Borders

Camellias are large shrubs
and perform best when
planted directly in the soil,
providing it is acidic. Before
buying camellias, check your
soil using a pH testing kit,
which can be bought from
most garden centers. When
planting, add some well rotted
garden compost to the soil,
and water new plants well for
the first year or two.

C. 'Lila Naff'

C. japonica
'Miss Universe'

Grow: Microgreens

Harvested as tender seedlings, microgreens are a fantastic way of enjoying delicious fresh salad leaves throughout the year. There are many types to try and, if you have a bright windowsill, they couldn't be easier to grow.

1 Sow the seeds into trays or pots filled with moist soil mix and cover with a dusting of more soil mix to the depth given on the seed package. Place the tray or pot into a clear plastic bag to help conserve moisture, then place it on a warm, bright windowsill. Check daily and remove the plastic bag when seedlings start to appear.

YOU WILL NEED
✻ **Materials:**
Seed
Soil mix
✻ **Equipment:**
Pot or seed tray

2 Seedlings grow quickly and most types will develop their first proper pairs of leaves just days after germinating. Keep them moist at all times, though there is no need to feed them.

4 To harvest microgreens simply cut them off at the base just above the soil and discard the roots. You can then refresh the soil mix and sow a new batch using the same method.

3 Microgreens are ready to harvest once they have grown two or three pairs of leaves, or are large enough to handle easily. Don't allow them to grow any larger.

Which to grow

Most leafy vegetables and herbs can be grown as microgreens, which is a good way of using up surplus seeds. For the tastiest leaves try:

- **Amaranth** (*below*), which has attractive red leaves.

- **Basil** and **cilantro**, which have an aromatic flavor.

- **Beets**, which are colorful with a fleshy texture.

- **Lettuce**, which produces mini leaves ideal for sandwiches.

Spinach 'Apollo'

Spinach

Tasty fresh spinach is a fast-growing crop that can be enjoyed for many months of the year if sown regularly. It is most commonly grown to maturity in the vegetable patch, but it can also be raised as baby leaves and microgreens in containers, and even on windowsills. The key to sweet tender leaves is to plant spinach in rich soil that contains a lot of organic matter, such as well rotted garden compost, and to water it frequently in dry weather. Dry spells can cause plants to "bolt" (*see right*), spoiling the crop, so water them diligently in summer.

Growing spinach

Sow the seed directly in the soil ½in (1cm) deep in rows spaced about 12in (30cm) apart. Thin the seedlings to leave 4–6in (10–15cm) between them. Harvest the leaves as soon as they reach a usable size. Pick them individually but let the plant continue to grow in place. Water the spinach after harvesting the leaves to help it to recover and produce more leaves.

AT A GLANCE
❧ **Plant type** Annual
☀ **Aspect** Full sun or light shade
◉ **Soil type** Fertile and moist
↓ **Sow seed** Early spring—late fall
◎ **Harvest** Late spring—winter

Growing advice

Spinach is one of the quickest and easiest crops to grow, and is ideal for smaller plots. Sow the seeds directly where the plants are to grow.

Harvesting baby leaves provides a quick crop that can even be grown in windowboxes. Sow seed and harvest the leaves after 2–3 weeks.

Spinach bolts and the leaves become tough and unpalatable if the soil gets dry. If this happens, quickly sow a new batch of seeds.

Magnolia x *soulangeana* 'Brozzonii'

Magnolias

Whether they are large and bowl-like or small and starry, the showy flowers of magnolia are a stunning sight in spring. This is a varied group of plants that ranges from compact deciduous shrubs to large evergreen trees, with varieties to suit all gardens. Although fully hardy, cold winds or frost can damage their blossoms, so plant in a sheltered spot and choose a later-flowering variety if you live in a cold area. Buy the biggest container-grown plant you can afford because it will establish better. Mulch regularly with garden compost. Keep plants well watered in summer—this is when the flower buds develop for spring.

Splendid spring feature

A magnolia tree in full bloom is an eagerly anticipated harbinger of spring. While choosing a sheltered site that will protect the tender blooms is important when deciding where to plant it, don't hide the magnolia. Bear in mind that you will want to enjoy its full, magnificent effect during those fleeting days when the tree is in full flower, so plant it where the blooms can easily be admired.

AT A GLANCE
- **Plant type** Hardy tree or shrub
- **Height** 10–70ft (3–20m)
- **Spread** 12–50ft (4–15m)
- **Aspect** Sun or light shade in shelter
- **Soil type** Moist but well drained

Which to choose

The classic magnolia, *M.* x *soulangeana* (*right*), bears pink or white flowers, and is best in larger sites. More compact magnolias are available.

Most magnolias have pink, purple, or white blooms, making yellow-flowered 'Daphne' something special. It grows to 12ft (4m) tall.

'Black Tulip' is another compact variety that is ideal for smaller plots. Its intense purple flowers can measure up to 6in (15cm) across.

Known as the star magnolia, *M. stellata* bears masses of dainty white flowers. It is compact enough to grow in a large patio container.

Broad bean 'Aquadulce Claudia'

Broad beans

Helping to fill the "hungry gap" in mid-spring when there is little else to pick, broad beans are one of the first crops to harvest. They are also easy to grow, and maturing early means they can soon be replaced with summer crops. In mild areas, seeds can be sown into small pots starting from fall until late winter for an early crop. Choose a variety suitable for fall sowing and protect the seedlings from cold weather with a cloche or cold frame. In other areas, it is best to wait until spring. Sow seeds into small pots under cover or directly outside, 2in (5cm) deep and spaced 10in (25cm) apart. When harvesting broad beans, pick the pods from the bottom first and work your way up the stem.

Good for the soil

Broad beans, also known as fava or horse beans, are delicious, especially when picked and enjoyed young. However, they are also useful for growing as a cover crop in winter to prevent soil erosion. The beans provide yet another benefit: once the crop has been cleared away, other plants, such as ornamental kale, will thrive on the nitrogen left behind in the soil by the broad bean's root system.

Growing advice

Once they are established and start to grow strongly, broad beans need only minimal care, other than regular watering during dry spells.

Provide support while the plants are still small, running stakes and string along the rows. Heavily laden plants can topple over.

Pinching out the growing tips when the first flowers appear helps to deter blackfly and encourages the pods to develop (*see p.188*).

AT A GLANCE
- ❋ **Plant type** Hardy annual
- ☼ **Aspect** Full sun, sheltered from wind
- ◎ **Soil type** Moist and well drained
- ↓ **Sow seed** Mid-fall—mid-spring
- ◎ **Harvest** Late spring—midsummer

Beets

Earthy, sweet-tasting beets are very easy to grow, and can be harvested as baby roots a few weeks after sowing or left to reach full size in about 90 days. The crisp leaves can also be enjoyed as a tasty cut-and-come-again salad ingredient, making this a good all-round crop for growing in small spaces, or even in containers. Sow seed directly into the soil starting in mid-spring in rows (*see pp.70–71*), and thin the seedlings to 4in (10cm) apart as they develop. Keep the seedlings well watered and remove any weeds that appear. Sow new batches of seed every four weeks for a regular harvest.

AT A GLANCE
- ❧ **Plant type** Hardy annual
- ☀ **Aspect** Full sun or light shade
- ◉ **Soil type** Fertile and well drained
- ⋁ **Sow seed** Early spring—midsummer
- ◎ **Harvest** Late spring—mid-fall

Which to choose

There is a large range of beet varieties to grow, which vary in size, shape, and color, and include unusual orange- and white-fleshed types.

'**Bull's Blood**' has firm and fleshy, deep red roots, and attractive dark red leaves that can be used to add vibrant color to a salad.

'**Chioggia Pink**' has bright red roots that, when sliced open, reveal striking alternating rings of attractive pink and white flesh.

Bulbs for
Spring color

No garden should be without bulbs, and time spent planting in fall will be rewarded with weeks of color in spring. Plant a wide variety in containers and beds to keep the color coming.

1 *Anemone coronaria* In shades of mauve, red, or white, these bulbs make excellent cut flowers.
↕ 10in (25cm) ◄ 8in (20cm)

2 *Anemone blanda* Flowering in shades of blue or white, these are a cheerful sight in early spring.
↕ 4in (10cm) ◄ 4in (10cm)

3 *Erythronium revolutum* Best in light shade, the pink flowers are held above marbled leaves.
↕ 12in (30cm) ◄ 6in (15cm)

4 *Puschkinia scilloides* Ideal for naturalizing or containers, it has blue or white starlike blooms.
↕ 6in (15cm) ◄ 4in (10cm)

5 *Fritillaria meleagris* With their checkerboard flowers, snake's head fritillaries should be planted *en masse* for the best effect.
↕ 12in (30cm) ◄ 4in (10cm)

6 *Scilla siberica* Suitable for planting beneath deciduous shrubs, it has bell-shaped flowers.
↕ 6in (15cm) ◄ 2in (5cm)

7 *Muscari armeniacum* Grape hyacinths quickly form natural clumps. Ideal for borders or pots.
↕ 6in (15cm) ◄ 4in (10cm)

8 *Crocus vernus* A carpet of crocuses create a spectacle in early spring. Plant in borders, rock gardens, or naturalize in grass.
↕ 4in (10cm) ◄ 2in (5cm)

9 *Hyacinthus orientalis* There is no mistaking the sweet scent of hyacinths, which flower in shades of white, pink, purple, or blue.
↕ 10in (25cm) ◄ 4in (10cm)

10 *Iris reticulata* These dwarf irises are among the earliest bulbs to emerge. Ideal for pots.
↕ 6in (15cm) ◄ 1in (2cm)

Swiss chard 'Bright Lights'

Swiss chard

One of the earliest, and latest, crops to harvest, Swiss chard is grown for its large leaves and crisp stems, and is cooked in a similar way to spinach. It is a stately plant with glossy foliage and brightly colored stems. Chard grows best in a rich soil with lots of organic matter dug into it. Sow seed thinly, ¾in (2cm) deep, in rows spaced 16in (40cm) apart. Thin the seedlings to intervals of 12in (30cm). Water them well during dry periods to stop the plants from "bolting" (suddenly flowering), and protect them with a frost blanket in winter. Pick the leaves individually (the oldest first) but let the plant carry on growing in place.

Decorative edible

Swiss chard is not only a versatile, highly nutritious vegetable, but it can perform as an ornamental plant as well, and looks very attractive planted alongside summer bedding. Its handsome ruffled leaves can also be shown to advantage by growing it among other vegetables or herbs with contrasting feathery foliage. Or, plant a ruby chard next to a plant bearing flowers that will complement the dramatic red ribs of the chard.

Which to grow

There is just a small range of varieties to choose from, each of which is grown in the same way. The colors and stem sizes are the only difference.

'Bright Lights' produces glossy, brightly colored stems in shades of yellow, red, or purple. The color may fade after cooking.

'Lucullus' has sturdy white stems that can be cooked like asparagus, while the leaves can be stripped and steamed like spinach.

AT A GLANCE
- ❀ **Plant type** Hardy biennial
- ☀ **Aspect** Full sun or dappled shade
- ◉ **Soil type** Fertile and moist
- ⌄ **Sow seed** Late spring—early fall
- ◎ **Harvest** Late spring—winter

Tulips

Few garden plants offer the sheer diversity of flower shape, color, and form as tulips. From simple, single-flowered types to the flamboyant parrot tulips, there are varieties to suit all gardens, and all are very easy to grow in beds and containers. Tulips are available to buy starting from late summer but are best planted during late fall (*see p.271*) to help avoid the fatal disease, *tulip fire*. When buying tulip bulbs, avoid any with signs of mold or damage. On heavy soils, add a handful of grit to the bottom of the planting holes. Once the leaves have died back after flowering, lift and store the bulbs until late fall (*see p.188*).

AT A GLANCE
- **Plant type** Hardy bulb
- **Height** 4–30in (10–75cm)
- **Spread** 2–4in (5–10cm)
- **Aspect** Full sun to light shade
- **Soil type** Fertile and well drained

Tulipa 'Golden Parrot'

Planting partners

Tulip varieties range in height from dwarf to tall forms, and can be planted with many other spring-flowering plants for a colorful display.

Dwarf spring bulbs, such as muscari (*above*) look effective planted alongside tulips. Also add crocus and dwarf daffodils to provide earlier color.

Biennial wallflowers are similar in height to many taller tulips, meaning they can support the tall blooms and provide an attractive backdrop.

Forget-me-nots are low-growing plants when young, and provide colorful ground cover and contrast beneath taller tulip varieties.

Choosing tulips

Taller tulip varieties are ideal for borders, where their graceful flowers are held above the neighboring plants, and where they can be sheltered from strong wind and rain, which can damage them. Shorter varieties are more versatile and are a good choice for the front of borders, or for containers and windowboxes. Smaller-flowered species tulips, such as *T. clusiana,* are excellent for naturalizing in lawns.

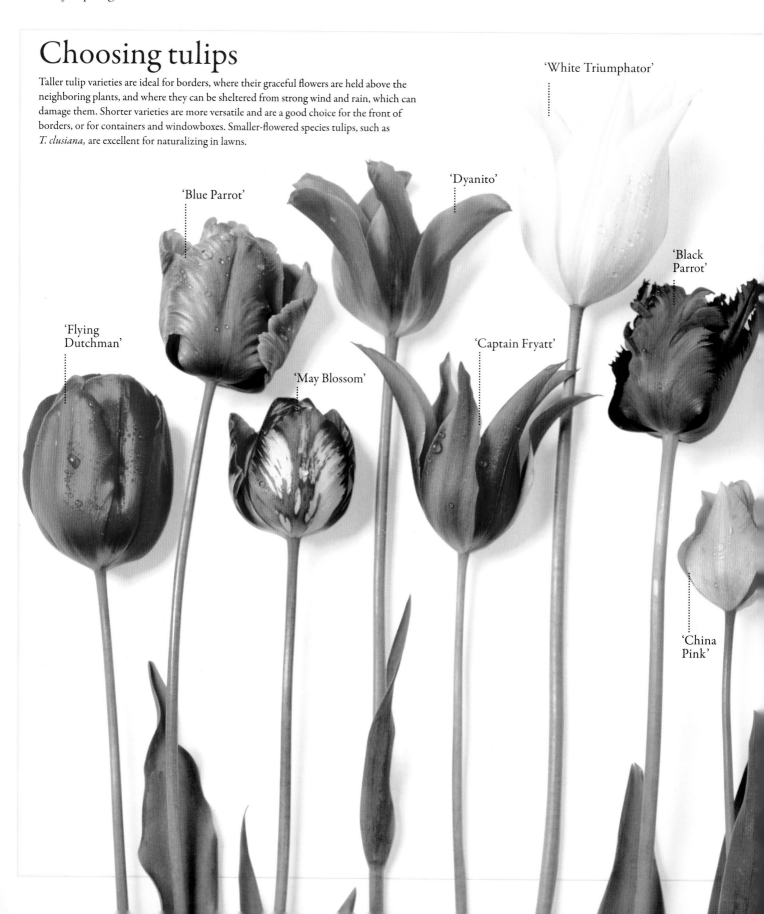

'White Triumphator'

'Dyanito'

'Blue Parrot'

'Black Parrot'

'Flying Dutchman'

'Captain Fryatt'

'May Blossom'

'China Pink'

'Asta Nielsen'

'West Point'

'Greenland'

Cut flowers

Tulips are easy to grow for cutting and should be picked before the flowers are fully open. To save robbing your borders of color, plant the bulbs in spare soil, such as in an empty vegetable bed, or in large containers. Once cut, discard the bulbs as growth the following year will be poor.

Indoor pots

For indoor displays, plant dwarf varieties into pots of soil mix during mid-fall. Set them outside in a cool, sheltered spot for at least eight weeks and regularly check the base of the pot for signs of roots. When roots show, bring the pot indoors into a cool, bright room, moving them to a warmer position once the shoots are 2in (5cm) tall. Keep them watered and they will flower within two weeks.

Patio planters

Most bulbs should be planted to a depth of three times the height of the bulb, and because tulip bulbs are quite large, they're planted deeper than many others. If planting bulbs in containers, start with the largest bulbs and plant in layers separated by compost. Bedding plants can be planted at the surface, which the bulbs will grow through.

Asparagus

Widely regarded as a delicacy, nothing beats the taste of freshly harvested, home-grown asparagus. Growing your own requires patience, however, because new plants take three years to produce their first crop. It is also a large plant that needs plenty of space, so is only suited to bigger plots. New bare-root crowns are planted in spring into well drained soil (*see below*). Keep them well watered and free of weeds during summer, and mulch them with well rotted garden compost in spring. Plants should also be protected from strong winds. After three years, you can harvest the emerging "spears" for about six weeks, after which you must stop and let the plants grow.

Planting asparagus crowns

Dig a trench 12in (30cm) wide, 8in (20cm) deep, and long enough to plant the crowns at intervals of 12in (30cm). Pour sifted soil down the center of the trench to make a mound that is 4in (10cm) high. Set the crowns onto the mound and cover with 2in (5cm) of sifted soil. As the stems appear, cover them with more sifted soil until the trench is full.

Growing advice

Once established, asparagus needs little care and will crop reliably for many years. The plants are only harvested for a few weeks each year.

Harvest the spears when 8in (20cm) tall, cutting them off 1in (2.5cm) below the soil surface. An old kitchen knife is ideal for this.

Let the plants carry on growing after harvesting then, in fall, cut the stems down to the ground. This will ensure a good crop next spring.

AT A GLANCE
- **Plant type** Hardy perennial
- **Aspect** Full sun
- **Soil type** Fertile and well drained
- **When to plant** Spring
- **Harvest** Late spring—early summer

Prunus 'Kanzan'

Flowering cherries

Festooned with blossom in spring, ornamental forms of *Prunus* make excellent garden trees. There are hundreds of varieties to choose from, with their flowers ranging from white to crimson, and from dainty single florets to large double confections, while some also have the added bonus of beautiful fall foliage, too. Many are ideal for smaller yards. Established trees need little care, but can simply be pruned in midsummer to maintain their shape or size.

A beauty all year long
While the flowering cherry tree is grown for its spring blossom and fall foliage, the shrub form of prunus is grown for its fall color, bark, flowers, or fruit. All types of prunus will grow in any type of soil, as long as it is never waterlogged.

AT A GLANCE
- ❦ **Plant type** Deciduous trees
- ♠ **Height** 10–40ft (3–12m)
- 🍂 **Spread** 10–40ft (3–12m)
- ☀ **Aspect** Full sun
- ◉ **Soil type** Fertile, moist, well drained

Which to choose

Double-flowered *P.* 'Kanzan' (*left*) gives a vivid show of large deep pink flowers from mid-spring. It has a broad habit, seen best in larger yards.

Upright and compact, *P.* 'Pandora' produces masses of single pale pink blooms in early spring. It is suitable for average-sized yards.

Weeping cherry, *P. pendula* 'Pendula Rubra' is ideal for smaller sites. It has an elegant arching habit and flowers in late spring.

Peas

Pea 'Ambassador'

Peas never taste sweeter than when eaten within hours of being picked from the garden. Easy to grow (even in pots), seed can be sown in rows in the ground starting in early spring, 2in (5cm) deep at 3in (7.5cm) intervals. These are climbing plants and require the support of stakes or plastic nets—set them up after sowing. Keep plants well watered and mulch around them to conserve moisture. Harvest the pods when the peas inside are swollen but tender.

Which to choose

The traditional peas are the podding varieties, which are shelled before eating. Other types include snow peas and sugar snap peas, which are grown in exactly the same way but are harvested slightly differently.

Snow peas are enjoyed "pod and all," instead of shelled. They are ready to be harvested just as the peas begin to swell inside the pods.

Sugar snap varieties are also grown for their edible pods—not the peas inside. Let the pods swell but pick before the peas develop within.

AT A GLANCE
- ⚘ **Plant type** Hardy annual
- ☀ **Aspect** Full sun
- ◉ **Soil type** Fertile, moist, well drained
- ⋎ **Sow seed** Early spring—early summer
- ◎ **Harvest** Early summer—late summer

Two directions of growth
While it is true that peas are climbing plants, low-growing peas that form a bush are also available. This means that if space is at a premium, you can grow your peas in two different directions. Let climbing peas scramble up a fence or a teepee, and plant the low-growing type to form a casual hedge surrounding a plot or bed.

Flowers for Spring scent

1

2

3

4

Spring is a season for heady scents, with many plants to grow that will fragrance the air on a sunny day. Some are pervasive enough to stop you in your tracks, while others require you to enjoy their charms at closer quarters.

5

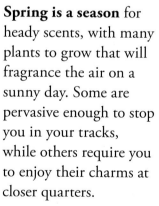

6

1 *Osmanthus delavayi* For sun or partial shade, this evergreen shrub has highly scented flowers.
🌱 12ft (4m) ◿ 12ft (4m)

2 *Viola cornuta* These violets have a peppery sweet scent. Plant them at the edge of a border.
🌱 6in (15cm) ◿ 4in (10cm)

3 *Choisya ternata* This evergreen shrub is known as Mexican orange blossom due to its sweetly scented white flowers in late spring.
🌱 8ft (2.5m) ◿ 8ft (2.5m)

4 *Primula vulgaris* One of the first spring flowers, the scent of primroses is best enjoyed up close.
🌱 4in (10cm) ◿ 4in (10cm)

5 *Polygonatum odoratum* The graceful flowers of Solomon's seal have a rich lilylike perfume.
🌱 20in (50cm) ◿ 20in (50cm)

6 *Daphne* x *burkwoodii* The scent of this evergreen shrub will fill the garden from late spring to early summer. Ideal for shade.
🌱 5ft (1.5m) ◿ 6ft (1.8m)

7 *Mahonia* x *media* This architectural evergreen shrub fills the air with its sweet fragrance from late fall to early spring.
🌱 10ft (3m) ◿ 10ft (3m)

8 *Viburnum carlesii* With its pink and white blooms, this deciduous shrub has a heady aroma.
🌱 6ft (2m) ◿ 6ft (2m)

9 *Corylopsis pauciflora* The bell-shaped flowers of winter hazel have a delicious cowslip scent.
🌱 5ft (1.5m) ◿ 8ft (2.5m)

10 *Erysimum cheiri* Biennial wallflowers bring a mass of color and scent to spring borders. They also make good cut flowers.
🌱 2ft (60cm) ◿ 1ft (30cm)

Rhododendron 'Sneezy'

Rhododendrons

A rhododendron in full flower is a spectacular sight, and is a sure sign of spring. This is a diverse group of plants, with thousands to choose from, ranging from knee-high shrubs to garden giants, and include evergreen and deciduous forms (most azaleas). They flower in a wide spectrum of colors, bearing simple trumpets to large corsage-type blooms, and many pink- or white-flowered varieties are scented. Some also have variegated foliage, giving them interest all year long. Most rhododendrons are fully hardy, though they prefer a sheltered site, while some early-flowering forms benefit from winter protection. All require acid soil, so check yours before buying. If it's alkaline, consider growing dwarf and compact forms in containers or in raised beds of lime-free soil.

AT A GLANCE
❦ **Plant type** Hardy shrub
⬆ **Height** 2–20ft (60cm–6m)
◣ **Spread** 2–20ft (60cm–6m)
☀ **Aspect** Full sun or dappled shade
◎ **Soil type** Acid, moist, well drained

Choosing rhododendrons

Some of the best for most gardens are the compact *R. yakushimanum* and *R. williamsianum* hybrids, which are ideal for borders or containers. Taller varieties can be very dramatic but since rhododendrons only flower in spring, you may not want to dedicate so much space to them.

Rhododendron decorum

'Ilam Cream'

'Nova Zembla'

'Vanessa Pastel'

'Furnivall's Daughter'

'Odee
Wright'

'Spek's
Orange'

'Purple
Splendor'

Planting partners

Pieris

These compact evergreen shrubs
bear weeping chains or upright
spikes of pink or white flowers
in spring. These are followed by
attractive red flamelike shoots.
Pieris grows in sun or part shade,
and needs rich, moist acid soil.
'Forest Flame' is widely available.

Camellias

These beautiful shrubs have
glossy evergreen leaves and
charming flowers that range in
color from white to dark red.
Most flower in late winter or
early spring, but some, such as
C. sasanqua, flower from late fall,
and are scented, too. They need
similar growing conditions to
rhododendrons—they like
shelter, dappled shade, and
moisture in summer.

Enkianthus

Producing pendent clusters
of pink or white flowers in late
spring, these deciduous shrubs
bloom just as rhododendrons
finish flowering. They also offer
further interest in fall, when their
leaves turn vibrant red. Plant
them in full sun or partial shade
in humus-rich, moist but well
drained, acid soil.

Lettuces

This salad-leaf staple can be grown and harvested almost all year, if sown regularly and given winter protection. There are two main types to grow: open-centered loose-leaf lettuce, and tightly closed crispheads. Both can be harvested young as a cut-and-come-again crop, or as whole, mature plants. Lettuce seed is sown ½in (1cm) deep, at 4in (10cm) intervals, in rows 12in (30cm) apart. They can also be grown in pots, which makes it easier to protect them from slugs.

AT A GLANCE

- ⚘ **Plant type** Annual
- ☀ **Aspect** Full sun or dappled shade
- ◉ **Soil type** Fertile and moist
- ⩔ **Sow seed** Early spring—mid-fall
- ◎ **Harvest** Late spring—mid-fall

Growing advice

There are many lettuce varieties to grow, all of which are sown and raised in the same way. The main difference is how you harvest them.

Crisphead lettuces, which include 'Little Gem' (*above*), are harvested as mature heads, cut off at the base several weeks after sowing.

Loose-leaf lettuce, which includes 'Lollo Rosso' (*above*), can be picked as individual leaves, letting the plant carry on growing.

All lettuce types can be harvested as baby leaves as soon as they are large enough. Take individual leaves or harvest whole seedlings.

Radish 'Rougette'

Radishes

This succulent and peppery root crop is one of the quickest and easiest to grow, and can be ready to harvest in as few as five weeks from sowing. Early crops can be started under cover by sowing the seeds in pots, thinning them as they grow, then planting them outside to reach maturity. Maincrops are sown directly in the soil, ¾in (2cm) deep, at ½in (1cm) intervals, in rows spaced 4in (10cm) apart. Seedlings should be thinned to 2in (5cm)—use the "thinnings" as a peppery salad leaf. Radishes are quick-growing and require little space, so they are ideal for sowing in containers and between slower-maturing crops (*see p.62*). For a regular supply, sow seeds every two weeks.

Harvest early and often

Radishes grow best in soil that is light, sandy, and out in the open, although summer crops are able to withstand some shade. Harvest and consume globe radishes as soon as they reach an edible size. However, if too many are ready all at once, allow the plants to run to flower— they will produce seeds that are delicious stir-fried, steamed, or used in salads.

AT A GLANCE
❀ **Plant type** Annual
☀ **Aspect** Full sun or dappled shade
◉ **Soil type** Freely draining
⋁ **Sow seed** Early spring—midsummer
◎ **Harvest** Mid-spring—late fall

Which to grow

Radishes grow quickly and should be pulled as soon as they are large enough to use. If left to grow for too long, the roots become woody.

Globe-shaped radishes are perfect for salads, and are often small enough to be eaten whole. Varieties include 'Cherry Belle' (*above*).

Cylindrical radish varieties, such as 'French Breakfast 3' (*above*), are easier to handle and slice for use in salads and sandwiches.

Syringa vulgaris 'Masséna'

Lilacs

Free-flowering and richly fragrant, these deciduous shrubs fill the air with sweet scent from late spring to early summer. Larger forms are a good source of cut flowers. Botanically named *Syringa*, the blooms range in color from white and purple through to dark red. Lilacs thrive in most soils and tolerate air pollution, making them ideal for urban plots. Mulch with garden compost in early spring and remove the faded flowerheads with pruning shears.

Which to choose

The common lilac, *S. vulgaris*, reaches the size of a small tree, and is best grown in larger yards. Where space is more limited, consider smaller shrubby species.

S. x *laciniata* flowers in late spring, bearing clusters of scented purple blooms. It grows to 6 x 10ft (2 x 3m) in height and spread.

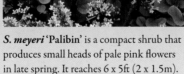

S. *meyeri* 'Palibin' is a compact shrub that produces small heads of pale pink flowers in late spring. It reaches 6 x 5ft (2 x 1.5m).

AT A GLANCE
- ☙ **Plant type** Deciduous shrub
- ⚘ **Height** 6–22ft (2–7m)
- ◣ **Spread** 5–22ft (1.5–7m)
- ☀ **Aspect** Full sun
- ◉ **Soil type** Fertile and well drained

S. vulgaris
'Katherine Havemeyer'

S. vulgaris
'Maud
Notcutt'

Carrot 'Mignon'

Carrots

This versatile crop is quick and easy to grow, and can be harvested as sweet and tender baby carrots a few weeks after sowing, or be allowed to reach full size. In addition to the familiar carrots with long orange roots, there are also those with round, purple, or white roots to try. Prepare the soil and remove any stones, which can distort the shape of the roots, and sow the seed ¾in (2cm) deep. Depending on variety, thin the seedlings to ¾–5in (2–12cm) apart. Protect plants from carrot fly (*see p.85*) and keep them well watered—dry spells can make carrots too tough to eat. They can then be harvested once they reach your desired size.

Long-term storage

If frost is imminent and you still have carrots in the ground, it is easy to harvest them and then store them indoors. Harvest the carrots, then twist the foliage off of each one. Arrange the carrots in a wooden box on a layer of sand. Cover with more sand and repeat with as many layers as needed. The carrots will keep for up to 5 months if kept in a cool dry place.

AT A GLANCE
- ❦ **Plant type** Biennial
- ☀ **Aspect** Full sun
- ◉ **Soil type** Well drained with no stones
- ⋎ **Sow seed** Early spring—late summer
- ◎ **Harvest** Late spring—late fall

Growing advice

Be gentle with carrot plants. Rough handling, or splashing them with water, releases their aroma, which will attract root-damaging carrot fly.

In smaller gardens, or where space is limited, varieties with shorter roots, such as 'Parmex' and 'Carson' can be grown in containers.

In the vegetable patch, carrots are ideal for sowing among rows of slow-growing crops, such as onions, making best use of the space.

Gooseberries

Tart and juicy, this is one of the earliest fruits to crop. Gooseberries are delicious in crisps, pies, and jams, and they also freeze very well for use later on. New plants are best planted during fall (*see p.274*), and can be grown naturally as bushes or trained up against a wall into space-saving cordons. In smaller plots, they can also be grown in large containers filled with all-purpose potting mix. Gooseberries are easy to grow. Prune them in summer and winter (*see p.191* and *p.302*), avoiding the sharp thorns that some varieties have. To protect the crop from birds, cover plants in spring with taut nets, secured to the ground.

Which to choose

Dessert varieties are sweet enough to eat straight from the bush, while sharp-tasting culinary types should be cooked. The fruits can be bright green, like 'Invicta' (*right*), or red, like Hinnonmäki Röd (*below*).

'Hinnonmäki Röd' (dessert)

AT A GLANCE
- ❧ **Plant type** Hardy deciduous shrub
- ♠ **Height** 3–5ft (1–1.5m)
- ◣ **Spread** 3–5ft (1–1.5m)
- ☀ **Aspect** Full sun or partial shade
- ◉ **Soil type** Moist and well drained
- ◎ **Harvest** Late spring—midsummer

Gooseberry 'Invicta' (culinary)

Jobs to do:
Spring

Around the yard:
- Protect plants from frost damage.
- Control weeds as they appear.
- Start mowing existing lawns or grow a new one from seed or sod.

In the vegetable garden:
- Sow vegetable seed directly outside and under cover.
- Harvest crops as they mature.

In beds and borders:
- Sow summer annuals from seed.
- Prune shrubs grown for summer flowers or winter stems.
- Plant summer-flowering bulbs.

Early spring

This is a busy time in the garden, with preparations to make before your trees, shrubs, and perennials come into full growth, and you can start planting new plants. Use these lists to prioritize what to sow, plant, and harvest, and the jobs to try to get done—weather permitting.

Essential jobs:

* Protect tender plants from frost using a frost blanket (*see p.69*).
* Sow hardy seeds directly into the soil outside (*see pp.70–71*).
* Mulch beds, containers, and borders with garden compost (*see p.70*).
* Deadhead bulbs that have finished flowering (*see p.71*).
* Sow tender seeds under cover in trays and pots (*see pp.72–73*).
* Order plug plants and modules to grow under cover.
* Prune shrubs that flower during summer (*see p.73*).
* Begin mowing lawns as they start growing again (*see p.74*).
* Prepare potatoes to plant (*see p.75*)
* Plant summer-flowering bulbs, such as lilies (*see p.260*).

Last chance to:

* Divide perennials as their new shoots appear (*see p.261*).
* Plant new deciduous hedges, such as beech (*see p.266*).
* Finish planting new bare-root deciduous trees, shrubs, and fruit bushes (*see p.272*).
* Prune fruit trees, including apples and pears (*see p.305*).

Continue to:

* Create air holes in the surface of frozen ponds (*see p.304*).
* Treat garden timber with wood preservative (*see p.306*).
* Warm up bare soil (*see p.309*).
* Provide water and food daily for garden wildlife.

Crops to sow:

Outside: Broad beans, parsnips, peas, spinach, sprouting broccoli, and summer cabbages and cauliflowers.
Under cover: Eggplants, beets, Brussels sprouts, calabrese, carrots, celery root, celery, chilies, kohlrabi, leeks, lettuces, microgreens, peppers, radishes, tomatoes, and turnips.

Crops to plant:

Broad beans, early potatoes, Jerusalem artichokes, onion and shallot sets, peas, and summer cauliflowers.

Harvest now:

Brussels sprouts, celery root, Jerusalem artichokes, kale, leeks, microgreens, parsnips, sprouting broccoli, rhubarb, and winter cabbages and cauliflowers.

Watch out for:

* Slugs and snails—control them using pellets or use organic techniques.

Protect young plants from frost

Cover tender seedlings with a frost blanket at night but remove it during the day. Weigh down the blanket at the edges but keep it loose so plants aren't crushed.

Mulching ornamentals

and fruit trees and bushes helps to suppress emerging weeds, retain moisture, and improve soil structure and fertility. Ensure that the soil is well watered first, then spread a layer 4in (10cm) thick around your plants, keeping it from touching their stems directly. Good mulches to use include well rotted garden compost, farmyard manure, and leaf mold.

Encourage bushy plants

by pinching out your seedlings. Once a seedling has a few pairs of full-sized leaves, remove the growing tip using your finger and thumb. This will ensure that the plant becomes bushy, with plenty of sideshoots and flower buds (*see p.91*). You can do this several times if the plant looks lanky.

Sowing hardy seeds outside

1 First dig the soil, then rake the surface thoroughly until it is fine and level. Using a dibber or the back of a trowel, make a shallow drill to the length required. Check the back of the seed package to see how deep to make the drill.

2 Sow seeds thinly along the drill at the spacing recommended on the package. Larger seeds can be placed more precisely. Fill in the drill with soil, and water the seeds using a watering can fitted with a rose.

Harvest the last of your winter crops while they are still good to eat. These include leeks, rutabagas, kale, parsnips, winter cabbages, celery root, chicory, Swiss chard, Brussels sprouts, sprouting broccoli, and Jerusalem artichokes. Once the bed is clear, remove and compost any plant debris, and get the soil ready to sow and plant summer crops.

3 Seedlings will emerge after a week or two, depending on type, and should be kept well watered as they develop. Pull out any weeds that appear at this time to stop them from competing with your plants.

4 As the seedlings grow, carefully thin them out so they aren't overcrowded and have room to develop properly. In addition, keep them well watered and weed-free. Thin them repeatedly as required.

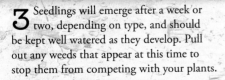

More jobs to do

Plants raised under cover need maximum light in order to grow strongly. Use a hose to wash algae, moss, and dirt from greenhouse or hothouse glass, and clean inside and out thoroughly with detergent.

While their stems are bare, this is the ideal time to tackle overgrown deciduous climbers and wall shrubs, such as honeysuckle. Prune the oldest stems to the base, thin congested growth, and shorten long shoots.

Deadheading bulbs not only keeps your display looking good but ensures that energy goes back into the bulb for next year. Pinch off spent flowers now but leave the foliage in place to die back naturally (*see p.188*).

Covering brassica plants with a net protects them from destructive pigeons that strip the leaves from newly planted cabbage, kale, broccoli, and cauliflower. To protect them fully, build a simple cage out of bamboo and cover it with a net or insect-proof mesh as soon as you have planted them. Pin the net into the soil to anchor it.

Sowing tender seed indoors

1 Fill a tray with good-quality, sifted soil mix and firm it down gently. Water it well using a watering can fitted with a fine rose, then let the tray drain. The compost should be moist to the touch.

Supporting taller perennials is easiest to do now while the new shoots are emerging, and enables the plants to grow through the support, hiding it. Simple frames made of garden stakes and string are effective, and can be easily adapted to accommodate tall or spreading plants.

Removing lawn weeds now will stop them from establishing, when they will be harder to control. Remove larger ones by hand or use lawn weedkiller. You can also apply high-nitrogen lawn feed to promote strong, weed-suppressing growth.

2 Sow the seeds thinly on the surface of the soil mix, following the spacing instructions on the package. Larger seeds can be spaced out individually; smaller ones are best lightly sprinkled.

3 Cover the seeds with a thin layer of soil mix to the depth given on the seed package. Don't be tempted to cover them too thickly—this may hinder them from coming up. Label the tray so you know which seeds it contains.

4 Place the tray in a warm propagator, on a bright windowsill, or in a greenhouse, until the seeds germinate in about 2–3 weeks. Keep the soil mix moist at all times.

Onions and shallots

can both be grown from "sets" (small dormant bulbs) now, for harvesting from midsummer to fall. Prepare the soil and plant the sets individually in rows with their tips just poking slightly out of the soil. To stop birds from pulling them up, protect the sets with row covers or nets while they take root.

Time to prune Many shrubs can be pruned now to promote flowers and growth.

Deciduous shrubs that

flower from midsummer onward, such as lavatera, are pruned now to maintain their shape and size, and to encourage flowering. Cut last year's flowered stems to within one or two buds of the older, woody framework. Water well and mulch afterwards.

Plant seedlings raised under cover into pots regularly to ensure growth. Look under their pots every few weeks, and if roots are visible, it's time to repot them into a container about an inch wider. Without disturbing the roots, ease the plant from its current pot, plant into the larger pot, and water it well.

Install support for climbing peas and beans before you sow or plant, because it will be tricky to do so afterward. Bamboo is ideal for tall climbing beans, and can be arranged in tepees or in rows. Peas are lower growing, and can be supported by nets, stakes, or a trellis.

Moving existing evergreen shrubs can be done now during mild spells. Water the plant the day before and prepare a suitable new hole. Working all around the plant, dig out the entire rootball, leaving it as intact as possible. Replant immediately and keep it well watered.

Start mowing the lawn on dry days once the grass shows signs of new growth. The first cut each season should just be a gentle trim—set the blades around ¼in (5mm) higher than your normal cut. Don't mow if the lawn is very wet. Trimming the edges will ensure it looks neat.

Planting early potatoes

1 Before planting seed potatoes or seed pieces, keep them in a cool, light spot indoors for 4–6 weeks until each one sprouts at least one "eye" about 1in (2cm) long.

2 Dig a narrow trench, around 5in (12cm) deep, where you plan to grow your potatoes, and spread well rotted garden compost or fertilizer in the bottom.

3 Carefully put the potatoes into the trench with the sprouted eye pointing upward. Space them about 12–30in (30–75cm) apart, depending on the variety.

4 Water the bottom of the trench thoroughly and cover the potatoes with soil. Shoots will appear in 2–3 weeks, and these will need protection from slugs.

Mid-spring

As the weather warms up, plants start to grow rapidly now, making this a good time to sow and plant, but it also means you need to spend time supporting and tying in new plant growth. Weeds will also be growing quickly now, so keep on top of them before they establish.

Essential jobs:

* Start hardening off plants raised under cover (*see p.77*).
* Plant new pond plants (*see p.77*).
* Grow new lawns from sod or seed (*see pp.78–79 and p.81*).
* Tie in climbers and wall shrubs as they grow (*see p.79*).
* Feed fruit trees and bushes with high-potash fertilizer.
* Plant new evergreen trees, shrubs, and conifers (*see p.80*).
* Tidy up borders before plants are in full growth (*see p.80*).
* Prune frost-damaged growth from evergreens (*see p.80*).
* Remove winter bedding plants as they finish flowering.
* Mulch strawberry plants with clean, fresh straw (*see p.80*).

Last chance to:

* Divide overgrown clumps of perennials (*see p.261*).
* Buy plug plant plants and modules to grow under cover.

Continue to:

* Protect young and tender plants from frosts (*see p.69*).
* Weed the garden regularly.
* Sow seeds (*see pp.70–73*).
* Deadhead spring bulbs (*see p.71*).
* Support growing plants (*see p.72*).
* Mow the lawn regularly at your normal cutting height.
* Plant growing seedlings raised under cover into pots (*see p.74*).
* Plant early and maincrop potatoes outside (*see p.75*).

Crops to sow:

Outside: Beets, broad beans, Brussels sprouts, carrots, kale, kohlrabi, leeks, lettuces, parsnips, peas, radishes, spinach, sprouting broccoli, summer cabbages and cauliflowers, and turnips.
Under cover: Eggplants, calabrese, green and string beans, celery root, celery, chilies, zucchini, cucumbers, Florence fennel, peppers, pumpkins, squashes, corn, tomatoes, and turnips.

Crops to plant:

Asparagus, early and maincrop potatoes, globe and Jerusalem artichokes, kohlrabi, lettuces, onion and shallot sets, peas, spinach, and summer cabbages and cauliflowers.

Harvest now:

Kale, leeks, radishes, rhubarb, spring cabbages, sprouting broccoli, parsnips, and winter cauliflowers.

Watch out for:

* Aphids—treat with pesticide or use organic techniques.

Hardening off plants raised under cover

acclimatizes them to life growing outdoors. Over a period of two to three weeks, set plants outside during the day but bring them in at night. If you have a cold frame, place them inside, only closing the lid at night. After this period you can then leave your hardened-off plants outside and uncovered.

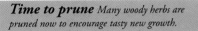

Time to prune Many woody herbs are pruned now to encourage tasty new growth.

Shrubby herbs, such as lavender and sage, can be lightly pruned. Remove the soft growth produced during last year, cutting back to new buds emerging on the older, woodier stems. Thin out weaker shoots and maintain a balanced shape. To prune rosemary, cut any weak stems back to strong, healthy new buds.

Planting new pond plants

1 Set the new plant in an aquatic mesh basket (*above*) of an appropriate size —the planting depth should be same as in the original container. If it's a tall plant, such as a reed or rush, place some rocks or stones at the bottom to prevent it from blowing over. Loosen the rootball gently.

2 Fill the basket with aquatic planting media. This feeds the plant without the nutrients leaching into the pond water. Don't use nutrient-rich potting mix as it encourages algae that turn the water green. Fill the basket to 2in (5cm) of the rim and firm the plant in.

3 Mulch around the plant with a 1in (2cm) layer of gravel to prevent fish from stirring up the media. This will also help weigh down the pot in the water and make it more stable. Water the plant well or plunge it into a bucket of pond water to saturate the planting media.

4 Gently lower the plant into its final position in the pond. Different types of plant need to be planted at specific depths, so check the planting instructions for each one. If you need to raise the pot in the water to achieve the correct depth, place it on some bricks or smooth stones.

**Check compost piles
and bins** and, if the material inside
is dark, crumbly, and sweet smelling, it's
ready to start using in the garden. Well
rotted garden compost helps to improve
soil structure, moisture-retention, and
ferility. Use it as a mulch (*see p. 70*) or
dig it into the soil when planting.

Buy bedding plants
while garden centers have the best
choice, and keep them in a frost-free
greenhouse or cold frame for now.
If you can't keep them under cover,
wait until frosts are less severe before
purchasing your plants, and cover
them at night with a frost blanket.

Creating a new
lawn using sod

1 Before laying sod, ensure the soil is flat, firm,
and well drained. Go over the area with a
garden rake to remove stones and weeds, then level
it off. Firm the surface down by treading on it.

2 Choose sod suited to your needs, such as
one that is hard-wearing. Roll out the first
strip using a long plank as a straight edge, then
roll out the rest, making sure the ends are
staggered. Kneel on the plank, not the grass.

Hilling potatoes helps to stabilize their stems, prevents the tubers from turning green by blocking sunlight, and encourages a larger crop. Starting once the new shoots have reached 8in (20cm) tall, regularly cover the base of the stems with soil all around until you have created a ridge 10in (25cm) high.

Tying in climbers and wall-trained plants as they produce new growth encourages them to cover the surface neatly, and means they are easier to prune. Tie new shoots to their supports once they reach 4–6in (10–15cm) long, tying them in again regularly as they grow. Leave the ties loose enough to allow the stems to thicken.

Planting crops under cover

1 Grow bags are ideal for growing crops under cover. They require regular watering, so to help retain moisture, make as small a planting hole as possible. Use a small plant pot as a cutting guide.

2 Before planting, make drainage holes in the bottom and loosen the soil mix to break up large lumps. After planting, water your plants well and provide supports as required.

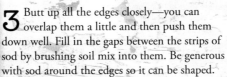

3 Butt up all the edges closely—you can overlap them a little and then push them down well. Fill in the gaps between the strips of sod by brushing soil mix into them. Be generous with sod around the edges so it can be shaped.

4 Trim the edges using an old knife or half-moon turf edger, bearing in mind that the sod will shrink slightly. Water it well, even if rain is forecast. Keep the area well watered for 3–4 weeks and try to keep off the grass while it establishes.

Tidying borders

while there is still space between plants is much easier than when they are in full growth. Use a hoe to remove weeds. Cut back spent growth, and clear away all plant debris. Doing these tasks will also help to control many plant diseases.

Planting evergreens

is best done during spring. When planted in fall, they are prone to damage caused by cold winter winds. Dig a generous planting hole and tease out the plant's roots. Position the plant, backfill with soil, and water it in well. Water regularly during summer.

Remove frost-damaged growth

from shrubs, especially evergreens, once the risk of hard frosts has passed. Prune damaged stems back to a healthy bud and pick off blackened leaves. To help the plant recover, mulch or apply fertilizer to promote healthy new growth.

Mulch around strawberry plants

to keep the developing fruits off of the soil. Traditionally straw was used (hence the name), but you can also use plastic strawberry mats. Straw allows good airflow around the fruits, which deters mold, while plastic mats are reusable.

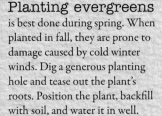

Sow a new lawn

1 Prepare the area by digging the soil thoroughly to break up any lumps and remove any larger stones. Then, rake the surface well to a fine tilth and level it off. If resowing an existing lawn, remove the turf first.

2 Use garden stakes to mark the area into 3ft (1m) squares. Measure out as much seed as you need to sow in each square, and scatter it evenly. The recommended sowing rate should be stated on the back of the package.

3 Lightly rake the seed into the surface. Water it in well using a can with a rose (*see above*). The seed will come up in a few days and should be watered regularly. Avoid walking on the lawn until it has established.

Time to prune *Many plants need pruning now to encourage flowering and healthy growth.*

Spring-flowering clematis,
such as *C. alpina*, *C. montana*, *C. armandii*, and *C. cirrhosa,* can be lightly pruned after flowering, once the last frost has passed. Remove dead and damaged stems, and trim to fit the available space. Tie in new shoots to their supports using string.

Shrubs grown for foliage
are pruned before growth starts but after the frosts have passed. For the best leaves, all stems can be pruned to the base, which may result in no flowers. As a compromise, cut some stems to the base, leaving the rest to flower later in the season.

Spring-flowering shrubs,
such as flowering currants, weigela, and forsythia, flower on last year's growth. When the plant has finished flowering, prune these woody stems down to just above the fresh green growth below. Leave new shoots that haven't flowered in place, as these will bloom next spring.

Shrubs with winter stems,
such as dogwoods and willow, should be cut back hard before their new leaves appear. Remove all growth, cutting it back to within two or three buds of the base of the plant. Although drastic, this promotes strong healthy summer growth and a good display of colored stems next winter.

Late spring

The risk of frosts will soon be over, allowing you to harden off and plant tender crops and ornamentals raised under cover. As the soil starts to warm up, seeds sown directly will germinate quickly, but more pests are active now. Take precautions and check plants for signs of early damage.

Essential jobs:

✱ Start trimming evergreens to keep them neat (*see p.83*).
✱ Plant tender vegetables raised under cover (*see p.84*).
✱ Take softwood cuttings from shrubby plants (*see p.84*).
✱ Ventilate plants growing under cover (*see p.85*).
✱ Install insect-proof nets over vegetable crops (*see p.85*).
✱ Lift and divide congested spring bulbs (*see p.261*).
✱ Tidy up spring-flowering perennials, such as hellebores.
✱ Thin out developing gooseberries to encourage larger berries.
✱ Hang codling moth traps in the branches of your fruit trees to avoid getting maggots in apples and pears.

Last chance to:

✱ Sow tender vegetables from seed under cover (*see pp.72–73*).
✱ Clean garden furniture.

Continue to:

✱ Sow hardy quick-growing crops directly into the soil (*see pp.70–71*).
✱ Stake perennial plants and taller bulbs as they grow (*see p.72*).
✱ Hill soil around potatoes (*see p.79*).
✱ Tie in climbers and wall shrubs as they grow (*see p.79*).
✱ Water crops and young plants regularly during dry spells.
✱ Weed beds and borders.
✱ Mow the lawn and trim the edges, removing the clippings.

Watch out for:

✱ Lily leaf beetle on lilies and fritillaries—squash them and their larvae on sight.

Crops to sow:

Under cover: Zucchini, cucumbers, green and string beans, pumpkins, squashes, and corn.
Outside: Beets, Brussels sprouts, calabrese, carrots, Florence fennel, kale, kohlrabi, leeks, lettuces, parsnips, peas, radishes, spinach, summer cabbages, sprouting broccoli, rutabagas, Swiss chard, turnips, and winter cabbages and cauliflowers.

Crops to plant:

Eggplants, Brussels sprouts, celery roots, celery, chilies, zucchini, cucumbers, early and maincrop potatoes, Florence fennel, globe and Jerusalem artichokes, kohlrabi, leeks, onion and shallot sets, peppers, pumpkins, squashes, strawberries, sprouting broccoli, summer cabbages and cauliflowers, and tomatoes.

Harvest now:

Asparagus, beets, broad beans, carrots, gooseberries, lettuces, peas, radishes, rhubarb, spinach, spring cabbages, strawberries, Swiss chard, and winter cauliflowers.

Pruning evergreens

Most evergreens need only minor pruning and are trimmed to shape as new growth appears. Any dead or diseased material should be removed. Prune spring-flowering shrubs after flowering has finished.

Grow plants from softwood cuttings

1 This type of cutting uses the new, soft shoots and can be used to grow most shrubby plants, including herbs. Early in the day, cut off pieces of nonflowering new growth, cutting just above a bud or leaf on the parent plant.

2 Using a sharp knife, cut the stem just below a leaf, making a cutting that's 2–4in (5–10cm) long. Trim the leaves from the bottom half and pinch out the soft tip. Dip the base of the stem into rooting powder to help encourage roots to form.

Start planting tender crops that were raised under cover, such as zucchini, tomatoes, squashes, pumpkins, chilies, green and string beans, corn, and outdoor cucumbers, in the garden after the risk of frost has passed. Be sure to harden them off fully first (*see p.77*), before planting them into containers or well prepared soil. Take measures to protect all young plants against slug damage.

3 In a pot, insert the cuttings into moist, gritty potting mix. Water them again and cover the pot with a clear plastic bag to retain moisture. Place in a light spot under cover and the cuttings will root in 4–6 weeks.

Covering crops with a fine net is an effective way to protect them from carrot fly larvae, which burrow into the roots of carrots, parsnips, parsley, Florence fennel, celery, and celery root, stunting their growth and ruining the harvest. Secure the edge of the net at soil level or bury it slightly to prevent the adult flies from crawling beneath it.

Frost protection material can be removed from tender plants once the risk of frost has passed. Keep it handy, in case a late frost is forecast and you need to protect any plants temporarily. Brush the material clean and store it away until fall.

Strawberry plants produce baby plantlets on long stems called "runners," which can be used in summer to grow new replacements (*see p.190*). Unless you want new plants, however, runners are best removed now to prevent the plants from wasting energy that would otherwise be used to produce fruit. Simply pinch them off with your fingers or cut the stems with scissors.

Ventilate greenhouses, cloches, and cold frames on warm days to prevent the plants inside from overheating and drying out. High temperatures now also encourage soft growth, which is easily damaged by cold conditions. Close the doors, vents, and lids at night, especially if low temperatures are forecast.

Summer

Signs of Summer

This is the most colorful season in the garden, with plants flowering and growing strongly, crops ready to harvest, and borders at their peak. The long, warm, and sunny days allow more opportunities to spend time in the garden, although dry spells mean regular watering.

Summer solstice

In the Northern Hemisphere the summer solstice occurs on or around June 21ˢᵗ. This is the point at which the Earth is tilted most closely toward the Sun on its annual orbital path. This results in warmer temperatures and increased light levels. If planning a new garden now, bear in mind that an area sunny in high summer may be shady at other times.

Day length

The summer solstice marks the longest day, as measured in daylight hours—days around this time typically offer 16 hours of light. However, as the Earth continues on its orbit, the days start getting shorter from midsummer. The solstice is also an important point for plants described as "short-day plants" (*see p. 91*), such as chrysanthemums and sedums, which will soon come into flower.

Weather

Summer in the US is filled with warm sunny days with a splash of rain tossed in for good measure. You never know what you are going to get for sure. July is typically the sunniest month of the year. The western and southern states typically have the warmest and sunniest locations. Our changeable climate makes it possible to grow a wide range of plants, but be sure to know your grow zone. Remember that the trick is to grow a variety of plants that enjoy different weather conditions.

Temperature

The average summer temperatures range from a high of 80° F (27°C) in Louisiana and Texas to a low of 52 °F (11 °C) in Alaska. Temperatures are generally warmer in the southern and western states. August is typically the warmest month, although not necessarily the sunniest. Daytime temperatures can remain high even toward the end of the season, though nights become cooler.

Plant science

Summer is the peak season for most plants to flower and produce new growth. This is when gardens are at their best, and there's a lot of science that makes it happen.

ANNUALS

Most summer annuals originate from habitats where events such as fire, flood, or drought are common, or where moisture or nutrition are short-lived. Their aim in life is to ensure the survival of their species, so annuals have rapid lifecycles, and often flower and produce their first seeds within weeks of germinating. With seeds produced, their mission is complete, and annuals then start to die, producing a brief display in the garden. Removing spent flowers (deadheading) before any seeds are produced forces plants to flower again to complete their mission.

Annuals flower and set seed quickly, and once enough are produced, the plants die.

Removing spent flowers before they produce seeds forces the plant to flower again.

PERENNIALS

Summer perennials will be coming into flower, and like many types of plant, this is influenced by day and night length. In a response known as "photoperiodism," many plants only come into flower once they have experienced a certain number of daylight hours relative to night. Flowering occurs when a trigger point is met, which depends on the species. Some flower before the summer solstice when days are getting longer, and are referred to as "long-day" plants, while "short-day" plants flower as the days become shorter after the solstice.

Special proteins in plants react to changes in day and night length.

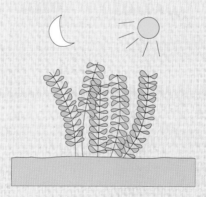

Plants flower when the right balance of day and nighttime has been met.

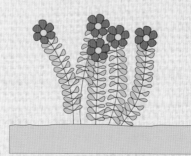

SHRUBS

Growth in all types of plant is controlled by a hormone called "auxin," which is concentrated in the main uppermost growing tips. Its role is to promote growth in the main tips and to suppress it in lower sideshoots. This is known as "apical dominance" and ensures that plants reach vertically toward the best light, which is essential for growth. Pruning plants or pinching out their main tips transfers the dominant effect to buds lower down, which then grow. The result for the gardener is shorter, bushier plants, with more flowering shoots.

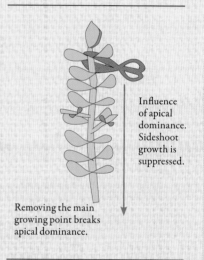

Influence of apical dominance. Sideshoot growth is suppressed.

Removing the main growing point breaks apical dominance.

On pruned plants, the uppermost sideshoots on each stem start growing.

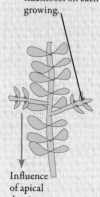

Influence of apical dominance.

If pruned, sideshoots also lose their dominance, causing them to bush out.

Allium giganteum

Alliums

With elegant blooms that look like lollipops
resplendent in shades of white, yellow, pink, and
purple, alliums are a distinctive sight in early
summer. Later, if they are left to dry, the spent
flowerheads can give interest during fall.
Alliums are ideal for beds and containers, and
are best planted in early fall (*see p.260*). The
leaves die back as the blooms appear, and after
flowering, the bulbs become dormant until spring.

Which to choose

The boldest alliums are those with large flowers and a lofty 3ft (1m) stem, such as
A. giganteum (*see right*), but shorter types can be just as colorful in the garden.

Dwarf species, such as the yellow-
flowered *A. flavum* (*above*), are ideal
for containers and rockeries. They
grow to as little as 4in (10cm) tall.

Mid-height species, such as pale
blue-flowered *A. caeruleum* (*above*),
reach 24in (60cm) tall, and are ideal
for the fronts of mixed borders.

AT A GLANCE
❦**Plant type** Hardy bulb
☙**Height** 4–39in (10–100cm)
🌢**Spread** 2–8in (5–20cm)
☀ **Aspect** Full sun or light shade
◉ **Soil type** Moist but well drained

Delphinium 'Tiddles'

Delphiniums

With their elegant, flower-packed spires of color, delphiniums are true stars of the cottage garden and herbaceous border. There are many varieties to choose from, ranging from the familiar blue ones, to white, mauve, and pink. These are tall plants, so place them at the back of the border, and stake them early to hold them upright. Dig in garden compost when planting, mulch afterward, and fertilize regularly for the best display. Cutting plants back hard after flowering often encourages a second flush of flowers. Delphiniums are prone to slugs, so take steps to control them.

Thinning makes a better display
In spring, delphiniums will produce plenty of vigorous shoots, but some of these may be gangly and skinny. Remove these lanky shoots when the plant is about one-quarter to one-third of its final size but leave the more robust shoots in place. Thinning out weak shoots enables the plant to focus energy on the strong shoots, which will produce larger flowers.

AT A GLANCE
- ❦ **Plant type** Hardy perennial
- ❦ **Height** 5–6ft (1.5–2m)
- ❦ **Spread** 2–3ft (60–90cm)
- ☼ **Aspect** Full sun
- ☺ **Soil type** Fertile and well drained

Planting partners

Delphinium flowers can be short-lived, so plant other upright flowering perennials among them to give borders vertical emphasis and drama.

Foxgloves, *Digitalis purpurea*, flower slightly earlier than delphiniums in sun or light shade.

Monkshood, *Aconitum carmichaelii,* flowers in fall, adding color to shady borders.

Foxtail lily, *Eremurus stenophyllus*, flowers at the same time as delphiniums, and is a good choice to grow alongside them in full sun.

Early potatoes

Homegrown potatoes are such a treat that digging them up feels just like finding buried treasure. Harvested in early summer, they leave you ample time to plant a later crop, reusing the same space right away. The plants are started as easy-to-grow seed potatoes (*see p.75*). Keep them well watered, and hill soil around them regularly (*see p.79*). Dig them up when the plants flower, gently working around the plant with a fork.

Container growing

Early potatoes can be grown in containers, and even in large sacks. A bucket-sized pot is ideal for one plant.

AT A GLANCE
- ☙ **Plant type** Annual tuber
- ☀ **Aspect** Full sun
- ◎ **Soil type** Fertile and well drained
- ⌄ **Plant** Early spring—midspring
- ◎ **Harvest** Early summer—midsummer

Border geraniums

Geranium 'Nimbus'

Also known as cranesbills, this diverse group of perennials is incredibly versatile in the garden, being free-flowering and able to cope with a wide variety of planting conditions. They come in a range of colors and sizes, fit with any planting style, and are ideal at the front or middle of a border, or as ground cover. Many are evergreen and some have interesting fall foliage. Geraniums grow well in most soils and need little care. Deadheading will promote a longer flowering season and, if clumps look ragged in midsummer, cut them back hard to encourage fresh new foliage, and sometimes more flowers.

Underplanting to enhance others

Geraniums are low-growing and have a shallow root system, so this makes them useful for underplanting. Planted underneath a tall flower-bearing plant, such as a rose bush, they provide a contrast in color, form, and texture, setting off the display of roses in bloom.

AT A GLANCE
- 🌿 **Plant type** Hardy perennial
- 🌱 **Height** 20–39in (50–100cm)
- 🌿 **Spread** 20–36in (50–90cm)
- ☀ **Aspect** Full sun or partial shade
- ⊚ **Soil type** Any

Which to choose

To been seen at their best in the border, choose species and hybrids, including 'Nimbus' (*left*), that grow to more than 20in (50cm) in height.

G. *pratense* has dainty saucer-shaped flowers in shades of white, purple, pink, and blue. Varieties include 'Mrs. Kendall Clark' (*above*).

G. x *oxonianum* is a vigorous perennial with a clump-forming habit. There are many varieties available with pink or red flowers.

G. *sylvaticum* flowers in early summer, bearing blue, white, pink, or purple flowers above lobed foliage. It forms attractive clumps.

Plant: Hanging baskets

Hanging baskets add instant color to the garden, and raise flowers to eye level where they can be easily enjoyed. They offer a chance to be creative and to try out new planting combinations.

YOU WILL NEED
★ **Materials:**
Hanging basket and fiber liner
Plastic sheet
Multipurpose soil mix
Slow-release fertilizer
Water-storing gel crystals
Bedding plants

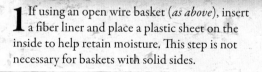

1 If using an open wire basket (*as above*), insert a fiber liner and place a plastic sheet on the inside to help retain moisture. This step is not necessary for baskets with solid sides.

2 Fill the basket with multipurpose potting mix to within 2in (5cm) of the rim. Mix in some slow-release fertilizer and water-storing gel crystals.

4 Add trailing and bushy plants around the central one, spacing them as evenly as possible. Cascading plants can also be threaded through the side of the basket. Use a sharp knife to make small slits in the liner and plastic.

5 Once the plants are all in place, carefully fill in around them with more potting mix and firm them in. Ensure the level of the mix is 1in (2.5cm) below the rim of the basket to make watering easier.

3 Position the tallest or most upright plant in the center of the basket, ensuring there is an even amount of space all around it for the other plants. To help the plants establish, tease their roots away from the rootball before planting.

6 Water the basket well and let it stand. If the potting mix settles and gaps appear between the plants, carefully add some more mix. Hang the basket in a sheltered position away from strong winds.

Strawberry 'Elsanta'
(summer-fruiting)

Strawberries

An irresistible taste of summer, strawberries are an easy fruit to grow. Choose a sunny spot with fertile, well drained soil, and plant them about 12in (30cm) apart. They also grow very well in containers and baskets, where their white or pink blossoms are as eye-catching as the berries. Varieties are divided into two main types depending on when they crop (*see below*). For the best harvest, it's worth planting both types. Replace tired old plants every two years.

Which to choose

Summer-fruiting varieties crop heavily from early summer to midsummer, while "perpetual" types produce a smaller crop from early summer to fall.

Alpine strawberries are an alternative to garden varieties. They fruit freely throughout summer, bearing very sweet and flavorsome miniature berries, and are ideal for growing in patio containers.

AT A GLANCE
- ❦ **Plant type** Hardy perennial
- ☼ **Aspect** Full sun
- ⊚ **Soil type** Fertile, moist, well drained
- ↓ **When to plant** Anytime if pot grown
- ◎ **Harvest** Early summer—fall

Clematis 'Victoria' (Group 3)

Summer clematis

Clothing a fence, trellis, or pergola with color, summer-flowering clematis are categorized according to when they flower and how they're pruned (*see p.197* and *p.309*). Group 2 consists of large-flowered hybrids that bloom in early summer, and often give a second flush later in the season. Giving two splashes of color, they are ideal for plots where space is at a premium (there are also compact varieties, suitable for containers). Group 3 clematis have smaller blooms borne in a single flush from mid- to late summer. It is a varied group, and includes varieties that are also grown for their seedheads in fall. Plant all clematis deeply and keep their roots cool, shaded by nearby plants, or by placing a large stone on the soil surface. Keep them well watered in summer, and mulch each spring for the best display.

AT A GLANCE
- ❦ **Plant type** Hardy climber
- ⚘ **Height** 6–12ft (2–4m)
- 🍃 **Spread** 3–5ft (1–1.5m)
- ☀ **Aspect** Full sun or part shade
- ◉ **Soil type** Fertile, moist, and cool

Which to grow

All clematis enjoy the same conditions, so consider planting varieties from groups 2 and 3 to enjoy the longest possible season of color.

Coming into flower by midsummer, group 3 variety, *C. tangutica*, has dainty blooms that look like lanterns, followed by seedheads in fall.

Group 2 variety, 'Bee's Jubilee', bears pink and white blooms up to 8in (20cm) across. Flowers in the second flush may be smaller.

Perennial
Kitchen herbs

Perennial herbs make an attractive addition to borders and containers, and provide an ever-ready supply of flavorsome leaves and shoots for the kitchen. Most are of Mediterranean origin, so prefer a sunny position and well drained soil. All are easy to grow.

1 Marjoram This compact herb has aromatic leaves and pretty pink flowers that butterflies love.
🌱 18in (45cm) ⬥ 12in (30cm)

2 Camomile Its scented foliage and daisylike flowers can be dried and made into a soothing tea.
🌱 4in (10cm) ⬥ 12in (30cm)

3 Rosemary This evergreen shrub has aromatic leaves and small blue or white flowers in spring. The leaves can be used fresh or dried.
🌱 5ft (1.5m) ⬥ 3ft (1m)

4 Bay This large evergreen shrub is suitable for borders or pots. The tasty leaves can be harvested all year, as required, and can be dried.
🌱 30ft (10m) ⬥ 30ft (10m)

5 Mint There are many varieties of mint, each with a distinctive flavor, such as chocolate or apple. It can spread, so grow it in a pot.
🌱 2ft (60cm) ⬥ 5ft (1.5m)

6 Thyme This low-growing evergreen shrub has aromatic leaves used in savory dishes.
🌱 12in (30cm) ⬥ 16in (40cm)

7 Sage This evergreen shrub has gray-green, purple, or variegated leaves, and small pink flowers. Use both leaves and shoots.
🌱 3ft (1m) ⬥ 3ft (1m)

8 Chives Grown for its mild, oniony flavor, its pink, globe-shaped flowers are also edible.
🌱 20in (50cm) ⬥ 4in (10cm)

9 Lemon balm Its attractive nettlelike, lemon-scented leaves are used to make a calming tea.
🌱 3ft (1m) ⬥ 2ft (60cm)

10 Fennel This tall, feathery plant is grown for its leaves and seeds, which taste of anise.
🌱 6ft (2m) ⬥ 2ft (60cm)

Turnip 'Atlantic'

Turnips

An ideal vegetable to grow in a small space, the tasty roots can be eaten young or mature, while the mustard-flavored leafy tops can be picked like collard greens, giving two crops in one. Sow seed where they are to grow (including in containers) ½in (1cm) deep and thin them to 6–9in (15–23cm) apart, depending on variety. Keep them well watered during dry spells to stop the roots from becoming tough, and sow new batches of seed every 2–3 weeks.

Growing advice

Turnip varieties vary from purple- to white-skinned, with rounded or flattened roots. Some mature faster, but all are grown in the same way.

Turnips are harvested 30–65 days after sowing. To enjoy them raw as baby roots, pull them once they reach the size of a golf ball; for mature roots to eat cooked, wait until they are tennis ball-sized.

AT A GLANCE
- ⚐ **Plant type** Biennial
- ☀ **Aspect** Full sun
- ◉ **Soil type** Fertile and well drained
- ⌄ **Sow seed** Early spring—late summer
- ◎ **Harvest** Early summer—late fall

Cherry 'Nabella'
(sour)

Cherries

A delicious summer treat, fresh cherries can be expensive to buy, but are now much easier to grow at home. Modern self-fertile varieties enable you to produce a crop with only a single tree (unlike most apples), while dwarfing rootstocks 'Colt', 'Tabel', and 'Gisela 5' limit their growth, making them suitable for smaller gardens. The smallest forms can even be grown in large patio containers if kept well watered. There are two types to grow. Sweet cherries can be enjoyed raw from the tree, while sour (or tart) cherries must be cooked with plenty of sugar. Once planted, cherries need little routine care. Mulch trees in spring with well rotted garden compost, protect the fruit from birds using nets, and prune the trees lightly in late summer to maintain their shape (*see p.197*).

Planting a cherry tree

A cherry tree must be planted in an open, sunny, but sheltered site with rich, deep, freely draining soil (note that sour cherry trees will grow in shade). Trees planted on inferior, shallow soil will yield small cherries with poor flavor, and will not survive as long. Plant trees in late fall, if bare-root (*see p.272*). Container-grown cherry trees can be planted at any time.

AT A GLANCE
- **Plant type** Deciduous tree
- **Height** 10–25ft (3–8m)
- **Spread** 10–20ft (3–6m)
- **Aspect** Full sun—shade (sour types)
- **Soil type** Fertile and well drained
- **Harvest** Early summer—early fall

Which to choose

Deciding between sweet and sour cherries is a matter of preference, but seek advice on the best dwarfing rootstock to meet your requirements.

Sweet cherries include the self-fertile varieties 'Brooks', 'Bing', and 'Sweetheart' (*above*). They bear fruit starting in midsummer onward.

Sour cherries are all self-fertile and will grow in shade. Varieties include 'Morello' (*above*), 'Evans', and 'Nabella' (*left*), which fruit in late summer.

Bedding plants for Summer color

Bedding plants provide long-lasting color in summer pots, windowboxes, and hanging baskets. You can also use them in bedding displays or to plug gaps in the borders. There is a large range to choose from, which can be grown from seed or bought as young plants in spring. Most require a sunny spot. For the best display, keep them deadheaded, and water and feed them regularly.

1 Petunias These can be low and bushy or trailing, and flower in a huge range of colors. Height and spread depend on type.

2 Ageratum This annual has fluffy blooms in shades of pink or blue, which are loved by bees.
🌷 8in (20cm)   ⬟ 10in (25cm)

3 Marguerites These shrubby perennials have daisylike blooms in a range of colors. They can be overwintered under cover.
🌷 12in (30cm)   ⬟ 16in (40cm)

4 Gazanias Best in full sun, their brightly colored, daisylike flowers close during cloudy spells.
🌷 10in (25cm)   ⬟ 10in (25cm)

5 Lobelia Smothered in white, pink, or blue flowers, this annual can be bushy or trailing. Height and spread depend on type.

6 Tagetes These free-flowering annuals bloom all summer, forming neat mounds of color.
🌷 10in (25cm)   ⬟ 10in (25cm)

7 Swan river daisies Low and bushy, this annual flowers freely in shades of white, pink, or blue.
🌷 10in (25cm)   ⬟ 10in (25cm)

8 Snapdragons Cottage garden favorites, these come in hues of red, orange, yellow, or white, and can be grown for cut flowers.
🌷 1–3ft (30–100cm)
⬟ 12in (30cm)

9 Zinnias These exotic-looking annuals provide color in late summer. They are good cut flowers.
🌷 1–3ft (30–100cm)
⬟ 12in (30cm)

10 Cosmos Easy to grow from seed, these are excellent in borders, and flower into fall.
🌷 2ft (60cm)   ⬟ 1ft (30cm)

Rosa 'Fragrant Cloud'

Roses

A must for any garden, plant species *Rosa* encompasses a large and varied group of shrubs. There are thousands of roses to choose from, ranging from compact varieties for containers, useful ground-cover forms, shrubby types for borders, to climbers and ramblers for walls and fences. Many are richly fragrant, others flower continually until the first hard frosts, and some also have decorative hips providing interest in fall. Roses are easy to care for. Simply mulch plants in spring, deadhead during summer, and prune them in fall or winter.

AT A GLANCE
- **Plant type** Hardy shrub/climber
- **Height** 1–40ft (30cm–12m)
- **Spread** 2–12ft (60cm–4m)
- **Aspect** Full sun
- **Soil type** Fertile and moist

Which to choose

Roses are commonly referred to as being either "hybrid tea" or "floribunda" varieties, which refers to their flowers and how they are produced.

Hybrid tea roses, like 'Poetry in Motion' (*above*) and 'Fragrant Cloud' (*left*), bear one large flower at the end of each stem. They are good for cutting.

Floribunda roses, also known as "cluster roses," produce a group of flowers at the end of each stem. 'Iceberg' (*above*) is one example.

Choosing roses

Roses all enjoy the same conditions, so deciding which to grow is a matter of taste. As a general rule, modern varieties flower more freely than old-fashioned types, and have good disease resistance. However, older varieties often have the finest scents. Rambling roses can grow very large, and bloom in a beautiful, but single, flush. Climbing varieties are less rampant but can flower throughout summer. Deadhead roses for the best show.

R. 'Complicata' (shrub)

R. 'Sandringham Centenary' (shrub)

Rosa 'Blush Damask' (shrub)

Containers

Roses grow well in containers as long as they are watered and fed regularly. Choose a pot at least 10in (25cm) or more deep, and ensure it has ample drainage holes. Miniature or patio varieties, such as 'Hand in Hand' (*left*) are the best choices. Plant in soil-based potting mix and position the container in a sunny site.

Ground cover

Some roses have a spreading habit, and either hug the soil or form a low mound, making them ideal to grow as ground cover. They are particularly useful for covering large or awkward areas, such as slopes. Varieties include any from the Flower Carpet series, like 'White' (*left*), or the County series, such as 'Worcestershire'.

R. 'Dorothy Perkins' (rambler)

R. centifolia (shrub)

R. 'Westerland' (shrub)

R. 'Ferdinand Pichard' (shrub)

Fall hips

If left in place, and not deadheaded after blooming in summer, the flowers of a number of shrub roses develop into attractive hips in fall, giving two seasons of interest. Good choices for colorful fruits are *R. gallica*, *R. moysii* (*left*), and *R. rugosa*, which have pink, red, or white flowers, and orange-red hips.

Climbers

Climbing and rambling roses are ideal for growing up vertical surfaces and over garden buildings. Rambling roses are vigorous, and best grown over larger structures, and even through trees. Climbing roses are ideal for fences, arches, and arbors, where their flowers can be enjoyed at eye level.

Garden beans

String bean 'Scarlet Emperor'

Green and string beans crop abundantly in summer—just 12 plants will be plenty for a small family. Being climbing plants, they are ideal to grow where space is limited, and can even be planted in large containers. Prepare the soil by digging in well rotted garden compost and provide support, such as a teepee of tall stakes. Seed can be sown into single pots in mid-spring under cover for an early crop, or directly into the ground in early summer. Tie the seedlings to their stakes at first to train them up, and keep them well watered throughout summer. When the plants have reached the top of their support, pinch out the tips to encourage bushy growth further down. Pick the pods while young and tender, and do so regularly to encourage more to grow.

Wait until the soil is warm

Beans are fast growing, so it is a waste of time to plant the seeds in cold, soggy ground. Wait until the last frost has passed and the soil is warmer than 60°F (15°C). Beans prefer rich, light soil and a sunny position. Plant the seeds 1½in (3cm) deep and about 9in (23cm) apart. They should germinate in 1–2 weeks.

AT A GLANCE
- ❦ **Plant type** Annual
- ☀ **Aspect** Full sun
- ◎ **Soil type** Fertile and moist
- ⌄ **Sow seed** Mid-spring—early summer
- ◎ **Harvest** Midsummer—early fall

Which to choose

Green and string beans are grown in the same way. Unless you have a preference between the two, grow both types on the same support.

String beans produce long, flattened pods that are harvested while young and tender, before the beans inside are fully developed.

Green beans produce slim, cylindrical pods. Pick them as soon as they are large enough to eat. Dwarf varieties can be grown in pots.

Viburnum opulus 'Roseum'

Viburnums

The summer-flowering forms of these deciduous shrubs are among the first to bloom after spring, and provide an elegant display of white flowers, sometimes flushed with pink. These appear as rounded globes or flat, frilly lacecaps, and they last for many weeks. Viburnums are large shrubs but many, such as *V. opulus*, also develop attractive berries and colorful foliage in fall, so certainly earn their place in the garden. They are easy to grow on most soils, and established shrubs need little care. Mulch plants in spring and prune after flowering has finished to remove any wayward stems, and dead, weak, or diseased growth.

Where to plant a viburnum

Viburnums are long-lived, so when planting one in your yard or garden, make sure that the location is thoughtfully chosen and the soil thoroughly prepared. If you would like to cultivate more plants, in summer, viburnums can propagated using softwood cuttings for deciduous species, and by using semi-ripe cuttings for evergreens (*see p.261*). However, viburnums can also be grown from seed in fall.

AT A GLANCE
- ❧ **Plant type** Hardy shrub
- ❧ **Height** 3–15ft (1–5m)
- ❧ **Spread** 3–15ft (1–5m)
- ☼ **Aspect** Full sun or partial shade
- ◉ **Soil type** Fertile, moist, well drained

Which to choose

Viburnum opulus gives interest in summer and fall, and is a good choice for most locations. 'Roseum' (*left*) has pretty blooms like pom-poms.

'**Compactum**' (*above*) is a dense, mound-forming variety, suitable for smaller yards. It reaches just 5ft (1.5m) in height and spread.

'**Xanthocarpum**' (*above*) bears white lacecap blooms that are followed by bright berries. These ripen to yellow from summer into fall.

Zucchini 'Defender'

Zucchini

This is one of the most abundant crops to grow, and you can look forward to harvesting 3 or 4 plump zucchini per plant each week in summer. They are also easy to grow but require a lot of space, so don't grow more than you really need (they can also be grown in pots if kept very well watered). Sow seed under cover in spring or outside in early summer, 1in (2.5cm) deep. Dig in plenty of organic matter before planting and keep the plants well watered. Pick zucchini a few days after they appear, while still small and tender. Zucchini crop rapidly, so check plants almost daily.

Pollinating zucchini flowers

In order to set fruit, zucchini rely on bees to pollinate them. In areas where there has been a sharp decline in bees, however, the buds begin to grow but then dry up or rot on the vine because insufficient pollen grains were delivered to the female flower. If low bee population is a problem where you live, you can pollinate your crop by hand (*see p.176*), and grow plants that will encourage more bees into your yard (*see p.152*).

AT A GLANCE
✹ **Plant type** Annual
☼ **Aspect** Full sun
◉ **Soil type** Fertile and moist
↓ **Sow seed** Mid-spring—early summer
◎ **Harvest** Midsummer—late summer

Growing advice

If kept well watered throughout summer, zucchini can provide three crops in one. Some varieties have a trailing habit—train them along the ground to keep them tidy.

Zucchini flowers are delicious stuffed and fried. Harvest the male, nonfruiting blooms, which are those without fruitlets behind their petals. Pick them in bud.

Yellow zucchini are easier to spot among the leaves, so you are less likely to miss any while they are still young and tender. They taste the same as green varieties.

Unpicked zucchini grow into large, thick-skinned marrow squash. They are a tasty crop, but are used differently to zucchini. You can also expect fewer per plant. To grow marrow squash, thin to 2–3 per plant and harvest in summer.

Raspberry 'Malling Jewel'
(summer-fruiting)

Raspberries

These sweet, juicy berries are simple to grow, and it doesn't take that many plants to yield a good crop. Raspberries are divided into summer- and fall-fruiting types. Plant varieties of each type to enjoy a harvest starting from midsummer until the first frost hits. Birds love the berries, so cover the plants with nets before they start to ripen. Water them well and mulch in spring with garden compost. The plants also require support and pruning (*see below*).

Growing advice

Raspberry canes require support as they grow, so plant them in rows next to two or three horizontal wires stretched between posts (*see below*). Tie the canes in to the wires regularly, using soft string.

To prune summer-fruiting raspberries, cut all fruited canes to the ground and tie the unfruited canes to their support. Prune all fall-fruiting canes completely to the ground in late winter.

AT A GLANCE
- ❧ **Plant type** Hardy shrub
- ⚘ **Height** 5–8ft (1.5–2.5m)
- ☘ **Spread** 1–2ft (30–60cm)
- ☀ **Aspect** Full sun or partial shade
- ◉ **Soil type** Fertile and moist
- ◎ **Harvest** Midsummer—mid-fall

Flowering plants for
Garden ponds

Ponds provide ideal habitats for wildlife, but can also be highly decorative, harboring colorful plants throughout summer. Aquatic plants also help to keep the water clear and healthy by shading the surface and releasing oxygen.

1 *Nymphaea odorata* With their showy flowers in many shades, waterlilies are planted in the pond. Position 6–39in (15–100cm) deep.
△ 6in–12ft (15cm–4m)

2 *Ranunculus flammula* This free-flowering perennial is ideal for planting at the pond margin.
↕ 28in (70cm) △ 30in (75cm)

3 *Mimulus cardinalis* The scarlet monkey flower is a colorful addition to the pond margin.
↕ 2ft (60cm) △ 2ft (60cm)

4 *Eriophorum angustifolium* Known as cotton grass, it bears fluffy white flowers during summer. It is suitable for pond edges.
↕ 1ft (30cm) △ 3ft (1m)

5 *Calla palustris* Best at the water's edge, it has large glossy leaves and flowers like arum lilies.
↕ 10in (25cm) △ 24in (60cm)

6 *Pontederia cordata* Known as pickerel weed, this marginal plant has spires of blue flowers. It is especially attractive to dragonflies.
↕ 36in (90cm) △ 30in (75cm)

7 *Typha minima* This miniature bullrush is ideal for the margin of smaller ponds. It has a tendency to spread, so plant it in a basket.
↕ 30in (75cm) △ 12in (30cm)

8 *Iris laevigata* This beautiful iris flowers in midsummer, and forms a clump at the pond's edge.
↕ 6ft (2m) △ 6ft (2m)

9 *Orontium aquaticum* Planted in the water, it has floating leaves and spikes of yellow flowers.
↕ 18in (45cm) △ 30in (75cm)

10 *Zantedeschia aethiopica* The arum lily has large glossy leaves and beautiful white flowers. Plant it at the pond's edge.
↕ 2ft (60cm) △ 1ft (30cm)

Lilium 'Venezuela' (oriental)

Lilies

These summer-flowering bulbs provide elegantly sculpted flowers, many of which are intoxicatingly fragrant, for several weeks in summer. Suitable for borders and containers, *Lilium*, as they are properly named, flower in a huge array of colors, from pure white to blackish red. There is also a surprisingly wide variation in the size, markings, and shape of the flowers. Plant bulbs in spring, keep them well watered once growth starts, and feed them every two weeks with tomato fertilizer. Taller varieties, especially Turk's-cap types, need support. Remove spent flowers and allow the foliage to die back naturally in fall.

AT A GLANCE
- **Plant type** Hardy bulb
- **Height** 2–5ft (60cm–1.5m)
- **Spread** 6–39in (15–100cm)
- **Aspect** Full sun or dappled shade
- **Soil type** Fertile and well drained

Planting partners

Lilies need to continue growing after flowering, so plant them near other plants that can help to disguise them, and also provide further color.

Verbena bonariensis is a tall, branching perennial that flowers from midsummer to fall. Grow it with taller lily varieties.

Montbretia, *Crocosmia* x *crocosmiiflora*, flowers in late summer and provides border interest after most shorter lilies have faded.

Choosing lilies

Lilies are mostly grown in a similar way, and there are four main flower types to choose from. Asiatic lilies have open, upward-, or outward-facing blooms, which are unscented. Turk's-cap types are sometimes scented, and bear abundant smaller blooms on a branched stem. Oriental lilies produce very large and fragrant flowers with broad petals, while the trumpet lilies are also highly scented, but have deep-throated blooms.

Lilium 'Star Gazer' (Oriental)

L. regale (trumpet)

In the garden

Lilies are fully hardy and can be left in the ground over winter as long as it isn't prone to waterlogging. If undisturbed, many lilies form clumps over time, which should be divided every three years to maintain their vigor (*see p.261*). Feed lily clumps by mulching them in spring.

L. 'Red Night'
(Asiatic)

L. 'Citronella'
(Turk's cap)

Cauliflower 'Tarifa'

Summer cauliflowers

This brassica is a great summer side dish, and is commonly harvested from midsummer to fall, although there are year-round varieties. While it is easy to grow, the plants are large and slow to mature, so this crop is best reserved for bigger plots with very rich soil. Seed can be sown in a prepared seedbed or under cover in modules, then transplanted to their final positions. Alternatively, buy young plants from a garden center. As the "curds" (the heads) form, cover them with some of the plant's own leaves to retain their pale color (*see p.195*). Keep plants well watered, and harvest them once the curds reach a good size.

Sowing cauliflower seedlings

Start seedlings indoors 4–6 weeks before the final frost. Once the weather is mild and the threat of frost has passed, you can transplant the most robust seedlings into the ground. Being careful to disturb their roots as little as possible, plant them 24in (60cm) away from one another in the row, and space the rows 24in (60cm) apart. A 10ft (3m) row should yield about 6 cauliflowers, but sizes may vary.

Which to choose

In addition to the conventional cauliflowers with white curds, there are also attractive colored forms. These are grown in the same way and can be used to add interest to cooked dishes.

Purple cauliflowers are rich in the same antioxidant that is found in red cabbage, and some retain their color once cooked. Varieties to try include 'Purple Graffiti' (*above*).

Romanesco cauliflower has unusual lime-green curds that develop into jagged peaks. It has a crisper texture than traditional varieties, and matures starting in late summer.

AT A GLANCE
- **Plant type** Hardy annual
- **Aspect** Full sun
- **Soil type** Fertile and moist
- **Sow seed** Early spring—mid-spring
- **Harvest** Midsummer—mid-fall

Sweet pea 'Spencer Mixed'

Sweet peas

These beautifully scented climbing annuals fill the air with fragrance, and are ideal for adding summer color to a fence or trellis. They are also an excellent source of cut flowers—the more they are cut, the more they produce new blooms. In milder areas, seeds can be sown under cover in fall to flower earlier; otherwise wait until spring. Pinch out young plants to encourage plenty of flowering stems, and water them frequently during dry spells. Deadhead any spent flowers regularly.

Which to choose

In addition to the climbing varieties, there are also dwarf forms that can be grown in containers.

The perennial sweet pea, *Lathyrus latifolius*, is as free-flowering as the annual forms and just as attractive. However, the blooms are smaller and unscented.

AT A GLANCE
- ❧ **Plant type** Hardy annual
- ♠ **Height** 1–8ft (30cm–2.5m)
- 🌰 **Spread** 12–18in (30–45cm)
- ☼ **Aspect** Full sun
- ◉ **Soil type** Moist and well drained
- ↓ **Sow seed** Fall—early spring

Globe artichoke
'Purple Globe'

Globe artichokes

Decorative as well as edible, these gourmet vegetables need plenty of space, but are attractive enough to grow in a flower bed. Best bought as young plants in spring, one should produce about ten edible heads in its second year. Globe artichokes are perennials, so will come back year after year. Keep plants well watered and free of weeds, and mulch with garden compost each spring. To maintain their vigor, divide the plants every three years (*see p.261*).

Growing advice

Harvest the flowers once the scaly buds are fully formed but before they start to open. They become inedible if left too long.

After harvesting, let the plants carry on growing until fall before cutting back the stems. Although hardy, the plants benefit from a thick mulch of compost over their crown.

AT A GLANCE
- ❧ **Plant type** Hardy perennial
- 🌱 **Height** 5–6ft (1.5–2m)
- 🍃 **Spread** 3–4ft (1–1.2m)
- ☼ **Aspect** Full sun
- ◉ **Soil type** Fertile and moist
- ◎ **Harvest** Early summer

Salvia x *superba* 'East Friesland'

Perennial salvias

Flowering throughout summer in vivid shades of white, pink, blue, and red, these perennials are an excellent addition to a sunny border. All of them have an upright habit and produce slender stems of tubular blooms that are a magnet for bees and butterflies. Some species are fully hardy but most are slightly tender, so protect these in winter. In milder areas, mulch around plants with well rotted garden compost or straw to protect the roots. In colder regions, lift and move them under cover until spring.

Growing salvia from seed

Plant salvia seeds 8–10 weeks before the last frost is forecast. Sow them in trays of moist seed-starting soil mix (*see pp.72–73*). To water the seeds, stand the tray in a large pan or basin of water to avoid disturbing the seeds by watering them from above. Transfer the seedlings to individual pots after they have produced their first two true leaves. Plant the seedlings outside in full to partial sun 10–18in (25–45cm) apart once the last frost has passed.

AT A GLANCE
- ❦ **Plant type** Hardy/half hardy perennial
- ⬧ **Height** 1–4ft (30cm–1.2m)
- ◭ **Spread** 1–3ft (30–90cm)
- ☀ **Aspect** Full sun
- ◉ **Soil type** Well drained

Which to choose

S. x *superba* is a hardy perennial bearing purple flowers from midsummer. Varieties include 'East Friesland' (*left*). It grows to 3 x 2ft (90 x 60cm).

S. x *jamensis* is a large shrubby plant that flowers in a wide range of colors. It requires protection during winter. Varieties include 'Hot Lips' (*above*).

S. *microphylla* flowers in late summer with vivid blooms like those of 'Robin's Pride' (*above*). It has a bushy habit and needs winter protection.

S. *greggii* is a low-growing shrubby perennial. There are many eye-catching varieties, including 'Navajo Cream' (*above*). Protect during winter.

Garlic 'Purple Wight'

Garlic

An essential ingredient in many dishes, garlic is straightforward and rewarding to grow, with each clove developing into a whole bulb. It is planted in fall and grows through winter, making it is easy to find space for it in empty plots, flower beds, or even containers. Plant the cloves directly where they are to grow, 4in (10cm) apart, with their tips just below the soil surface. Cover with cloches or a frost blanket in frosty weather, and keep plants well watered during dry weather as the bulbs form. Harvest in midsummer, once the leaves have turned yellow, carefully digging up the bulbs with a fork. The bulbs can then be dried and braided for storage (*see pp.146–147* and *p.194*).

Natural fungicide

Garlic enjoys a folk reputation for warding off evil, but in the garden it can help deter fungus and pests. Because garlic accumulates sulfur, a naturally occurring fungicide, planting it throughout the garden will protect other plants from attack. In addition, garlic planted near lettuce will help deter aphids. There is an exception, however, because garlic planted near beans or peas will stunt their growth.

AT A GLANCE
- ❧ **Plant type** Hardy annual
- ☼ **Aspect** Full sun
- ☉ **Soil type** Well drained
- ⌄ **Plant cloves** Mid-fall—winter
- ◎ **Harvest** Early summer—late summer

Growing advice

Only buy bulbs certified for planting. Bulbs sold in supermarkets are sometimes treated with sprout inhibitor, and therefore won't grow.

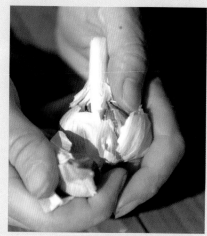

Garlic bulbs are supplied whole. Divide the bulb into individual cloves for planting, but avoid damaging the outer skins of the cloves.

Plant into small pots if local conditions are unfavorable. Allow them to take root, then plant them outside when the weather allows.

Climbers for Vertical color

Flowering climbers provide drama, color, and scent to the garden, and are invaluable for covering ugly fences or walls. Some, such as passion flower, are self-clinging and attach themselves to surfaces while many others, including honeysuckle, need regular training and tying in to keep them tidy.

1 *Schizophragma integrifolium* The Chinese hydrangea vine has showy white flowers, and is ideal for a shady wall or fence, or an old tree.
🌱 30ft (10m) ◀ 12ft (4m)

2 *Jasminum officinale* Jasmine has wonderfully scented white flowers. It needs a warm position.
🌱 10ft (3m) ◀ 8ft (2.5m)

3 *Thunbergia alata* Annual black-eyed Susan will quickly cover a trellis or obelisk in color.
🌱 8ft (2.5m) ◀ 3ft (1m)

4 *Trachelospermum jasminoides* An evergreen with richly scented flowers, it needs warmth and shelter.
🌱 25ft (8m) ◀ 25ft (8m)

5 *Eccremocarpus scaber* Exotic-looking Chilean glory is tender but grows quickly. It can be grown from seed and treated as an annual.
🌱 10ft (3m) ◀ 3ft (1m)

6 *Passiflora caerulea* The hardy passion flower has eye-catching blooms in summer followed by decorative orange fruits in fall.
🌱 15ft (5m) ◀ 12ft (4m)

7 *Wisteria floribunda* Bearing chains of fragrant flowers, this vigorous shrub needs something sturdy to climb, and ample space.
🌱 28ft (9m) ◀ 5ft (1.5m)

8 *Ipomoea purpurea* Annual morning glory is grown from seed, and flowers abundantly in sun.
🌱 8ft (2.5m) ◀ 6ft (2m)

9 *Tropaeolum majus* Grown from seed, annual nasturtiums trail or climb, and flower very freely.
🌱 6ft (1.8m) ◀ 6ft (1.8m)

10 *Lonicera periclymenum* Fragrant honeysuckle is a great choice for a wall or a fence in a cottage or wildlife garden.
🌱 22ft (7m) ◀ 5ft (1.5m)

Shallot 'Golden Gourmet'

Onions and shallots

Onions and shallots are kitchen essentials and are very easy to grow. They're usually raised from sets (small bulbs) planted in early spring (*see p.73*). Each onion set grows into a larger bulb, while a shallot set produces 6–8 shallots. Plant onions 4in (10cm) apart, shallots 10in (25cm) apart, with their tips set just above the soil surface. Weed regularly and water during dry spells. Harvest when the leafy tops have turned yellow and start to flop over (*see p.194*).

Which to choose

Onions are larger than shallots and grow as individual bulbs (*see below*). They have a stronger flavor, and have either red or white flesh.

Shallots develop as small clusters of bulbs (*see right*) that are harvested together but then separated. The bulbs can be round or torpedo-shaped, and some varieties have pink-tinged flesh.

AT A GLANCE
- ❧ **Plant type** Hardy biennial
- ☀ **Aspect** Full sun
- ◎ **Soil type** Well drained
- ⌄ **Plant sets** Early spring—late spring
- ◎ **Harvest** Midsummer—mid-fall

Make: A garlic braid

Braiding garlic is a traditional method of storing homegrown bulbs. To make a braid you will need at least ten bulbs, complete with their stems, which have been cleaned and dried for two to four weeks.

1 Trim the roots and brush the bulbs clean. On a flat surface, set the first stem in the center with two others on top, one pointing to the left, the other to the right (*see above*).

3 When all the bulbs have been added, divide the stems on the left, right, and center of the braid into three strands. Try to avoid disturbing the cluster of bulbs at this stage.

2 Set three more bulbs onto the first trio, again crossing over the central stem pointing left, then right. Keep adding stems, alternating the direction they are pointing.

4 Braid the stems, passing the strands right-over-center, then left-over-center until the whole stem is braided. Apply an even tension for a neat finish, and tie the loose ends into a knot.

HELPFUL TIP

The best garlic for braiding are "softneck" varieties. These can be stored for longer than "hardneck" types, and have pliable stems that are more easily bent into braids.

5 Hang the braid in a cool, airy place, like a shed, for 2–3 weeks to let the bulb skins and stems dry out. It can then be brought indoors to use as required.

Red, white, and black currants

Red currant
'Jonkheer van Tets'

Whichever color you prefer, currants crop prolifically once established, bearing sweet, sharp-tasting berries starting from midsummer. Just one or two plants can provide all the fruit you need, which can be eaten raw or used in cooking. Keep plants well watered and mulch with well rotted garden compost in spring. To deter birds, cover the plants with nets before the currants start to ripen, or the fruit will soon vanish. To encourage fruiting, prune plants in summer and winter (*see p.191*).

A hedge of red currants

Botanically speaking, there are only two kinds of currants, because the white currant is only a variant of the red. Black currants tend to grow into substantial, spreading bushes. Red or white currants, however, can be trained to grow as a hedge, and could be used as a divider or partition around a vegetable bed.

AT A GLANCE
- ❧ **Plant type** Hardy shrub
- ♠ **Height** 5–6ft (1.5–2m)
- ◤ **Spread** 5–6ft (1.5–2m)
- ☼ **Aspect** Full sun or partial shade
- ◉ **Soil type** Fertile and free draining
- ◎ **Harvest** Midsummer—late summer

White currant
'Versailles Blanche'

Black currant
'Ben Lomond'

Growing advice

Although they are closely related, black currants are planted and cared for slightly differently than red or white currants.

To plant black currants, plant the crown below soil level. Red and white currants are planted proud of the soil surface.

Black currant bushes become laden with berries, which can damage younger fruiting stems. Insert stakes for support.

Modern black currants, such as those with "Ben" is their name, ripen as whole "sprigs" (*above*), which makes picking them easy. Older varieties are harvested as individual berries.

Cabbage 'Greyhound'

Summer Cabbages

This is a tasty and versatile vegetable that can be harvested throughout summer and fall. It grows slowly, however, and requires a lot of space, so is best reserved for larger plots. Sow seed into a seedbed or in trays under cover, before transplanting the young plants to their final positions, 12–18in (30–45cm) apart, in early summer. Keep the plants watered well and, once they reach a usable size, harvest the heads by cutting through the stem.

Growing advice

Cover plants with insect mesh after planting to protect them from attack by birds and the caterpillars of cabbage-white butterflies.

If left in the ground after harvesting, cabbage stumps may resprout. Encourage this by cutting a cross in the cut end.

AT A GLANCE
* **Plant type** Hardy biennial
* **Aspect** Partial shade
* **Soil type** Fertile and moist
* **Sow seed** Early spring—late spring
* **Harvest** Late summer—late fall

Plants to attract
Bees and butterflies

Bees and butterflies play a vital role in the garden, pollinating flowers and enabling crops to set their fruit. They are also highly attractive, bringing natural sound, color, and life. To encourage them into your garden, grow plants rich in nectar with simple, colorful blooms that are highly visible and allow insects easy access.

1 *Limnanthes douglasii* Annual poached-egg plant grows very quickly from seed and flowers freely.
🌱 6in (15cm) ◣ 6in (15cm)

2 *Echinacea purpurea* This attractive perennial has pink or yellow flowers starting in midsummer.
🌱 3ft (1m) ◣ 2ft (60cm)

3 *Centaurea montana* Perennial knapweed bears spidery blue flowers from early to midsummer.
🌱 18in (45cm) ◣ 24in (60cm)

4 *Buddleja davidii* Known as butterfly bush, this vigorous shrub is by far the best plant you can grow to attract butterflies.
🌱 12ft (4m) ◣ 12ft (4m)

5 *Monarda didyma* Known as bee balm, this perennial has white, red, or pink summer flowers, with many varieties to choose from.
🌱 3ft (90cm) ◣ 18in (45cm)

6 *Campanula persicifolia* This evergreen perennial bears dainty bell-shaped blooms in early summer.
🌱 3ft (90cm) ◣ 1ft (30cm)

7 *Calendula officinalis* Annual pot marigolds are excellent for cutting. The edible flowers are good in salads.
🌱 18in (45cm) ◣ 12in (30cm)

8 *Verbena bonariensis* This tall, graceful perennial flowers all summer on elegant wiry stems.
🌱 3ft (1m) ◣ 1ft (30cm)

9 *Echinops ritro* Globe thistle is a large upright perennial, and a good source of flowers for cutting.
🌱 3ft (90cm) ◣ 2ft (60cm)

10 *Cephalaria gigantea* Ideal for the back of a border, this imposing perennial has branching stems of yellow flowers. Bees love it.
🌱 6ft (1.8m) ◣ 3ft (1m)

Cucumber 'Burpless Tasty Green'

Cucumbers

A key ingredient in a summer salad, the succulent cucumber is available as a smooth-skinned greenhouse variety or as an outdoor "ridge" type, with textured skin. Greenhouse varieties are climbers, and are trained up stakes or strings. Once they reach the top, pinch out their tips. When the cucumbers begin to develop, pinch out the end of each sideshoot, leaving two leaves after each cucumber. Outdoor types are planted directly in the soil, and can either sprawl across the ground or be trained up supports to save space. To promote fruiting, pinch out the main stem after seven leaves have formed. Water them generously and feed weekly with tomato fertilizer.

Tips for successful cropping

Cucumbers prefer rich soil, so dig plenty of well rotted garden compost or manure into the bed before planting. Seeds can be started inside under cover (*see p.72*) a month before the final frost. Or, in early summer, sow them 1in (2cm) deep, 24in (60cm) apart directly outside. The plants consume high levels of water and must never be allowed to dry out otherwise they may fail to develop a crop.

AT A GLANCE
- ☙ **Plant type** Annual
- ☀ **Aspect** Full sun
- ◉ **Soil type** Fertile and moist
- ⋁ **Sow seed** Mid-spring—early summer
- ◎ **Harvest** Midsummer—mid-fall

Growing advice

Greenhouse and outdoor cucumbers have different growth habits and differing crops, but some tasks are common to growing both types.

Male flowers are not required and should be removed as they appear. These are the blooms that don't have a fruitlet behind their petals.

Harvest cucumbers once they reach a usable size but are still tender. Cut through the tough stalk using scissors or pruning shears.

Fuchsia 'Heidi Ann'

Fuschias

These colorful shrubs have beautiful, long-lasting flowers and are easy to grow, making them very popular. There is a huge range of varieties, from tender bedding plants for pots and hanging baskets, to hardy shrubs to grow in the border—some can even be used as a hedge. Offer them shade in the hottest part of the day, water them generously, and shelter them from cold winds. Tender varieties should be brought under cover in fall. If you don't have space for mature plants indoors, take semi-ripe cuttings in summer (*see pp.194–195*) to bring inside. In colder areas, hardy fuchsias benefit from being mulched with garden compost during fall to help protect their roots.

Caring for fuchsias indoors and out

Where temperatures are consistently above 41°F (5°C), deciduous fuchsias will remain evergreen. However, if they are exposed to temperatures below this level in winter, the top growth may die off. If this happens, cut the fuchsia back to the ground in spring to allow the plant to start again. In a greenhouse or porch, fuchsias need high-nitrogen feeds and plenty of potash when in flower.

AT A GLANCE

❦ **Plant type** Hardy/half hardy shrub
🌱 **Height** 6in–6ft (15cm–2m)
🌿 **Spread** 1–5ft (30cm–1.5m)
☼ **Aspect** Full sun or dappled shade
◉ **Soil type** Fertile, moist, well drained

Which to choose

Hardy fuchsias make excellent border shrubs and will flower for weeks, but their blooms are small and simple compared to the tender hybrids. These require winter protection under cover, however.

Hardy fuchsias include individually named hybrids, such as 'Heidi Ann' (*left*), and the many varieties of *F. magellanica* (*above*).

Tender fuchsias flower in a wider range of colors and styles than hardy types. 'Orange King' (*above*) is a trailing form for baskets.

Tomato 'Gardener's Delight'

Tomatoes

From cherry-sized to large beefsteaks, this is one of the most popular crops to grow. There are hundreds to choose, from the latest hybrids to fascinating "heirloom" tomatoes. All require sunlight and warmth to crop well, and are ideal for greenhouses and growing frames, though some can also be grown outside in bright, sheltered spots. Plant them directly into the soil or into grow bags or pots. Tomatoes can be grown from seed in spring, which gives the best range of varieties, or bought as young plants. Keep them well watered and feed them with high-potash tomato fertilizer every week once the first flowers appear. Plants can crop freely, so check them daily for the best harvest.

AT A GLANCE
- ⚘ **Plant type** Annual
- ☼ **Aspect** Full sun
- ◉ **Soil type** Fertile and moist
- ⋁ **Sow seed** Early spring—mid-spring
- ◎ **Harvest** Midsummer—mid-fall

'Golden Pearl'
(cherry)

'Whipper Snapper'
(cherry)

Choosing tomatoes

Tomatoes are divided into two groups, cordon and bush varieties. Cordon varieties
are trained as a single stem *(see right)* and are usually grown under cover. Bush
varieties have multiple stems and are commonly grown outside. The fruits range
greatly in color, size, flavor, and fleshiness. Choose the right type for your garden,
and a variety that suits your taste.

'Beefeater'
(beefsteak)

'Ananas Noire'
(heirloom)

'Gardener's Delight'
(large cherry)

Growing advice

Supporting

Cordon tomatoes are grown as a single stem supported by a stake or vertical string. Provide the support when the tomato is first planted and tie the stem to it as it grows. If using a string support, carefully wind the stem around it. Bush tomatoes have many stems that will all need support. Insert as many stakes as are necessary and tie the stems to them.

Sideshoots

Tomatoes naturally produce sideshoots at the joints between their main stems and leaf stalks. On bush types, these are allowed to develop and require support (*see above*). When growing cordon varieties, pinch out any sideshoots that form while they are still small. Also remove their main growing tip once the plant reaches the top of its support (*see p.195*).

Harvesting

Tomatoes quickly spoil if left on the plant too long, so harvest them regularly, and don't rely on their shade to indicate ripeness. Even though most tomatoes ripen red, others turn yellow, green, or black. A tomato is ready to pick as soon as you can pull it easily from the truss at the "knuckle." This is the swollen bump on the stem where the fruit is attached.

Plum 'Victoria'
(dual-purpose)

Plums

A delightful feature in the garden, a plum tree provides pretty blossoms in spring and an abundant summer harvest. Varieties are either culinary or dessert types, but a few are dual-purpose, suitable for cooking and eating raw. Many are also self-fertile and available on dwarfing rootstocks so, even if you only have space available for one tree, you will be able to enjoy a crop of plums. For the best harvest, position the tree in a sheltered spot to protect the blossom from frost. Mulch in spring with compost, and in summer, thin out the young plums (*see p.193*). The plums are ready to be picked when soft and ripe. After harvesting the fruit, you can prune the tree (*see p.197*).

Consider the climate

When choosing a plum tree for your garden, bear in mind your local climate. Certain plum cultivars need a fairly long, cold winter in order to bear fruit. This means these trees come into flower later, which gives the blossoms a better chance of avoiding being destroyed by any late frosts than those types that come into bloom earlier in spring.

AT A GLANCE

- ❦ **Plant type** Hardy deciduous tree
- ⚘ **Height** 6–10ft (2–3m)
- ⛰ **Spread** 6–10ft (2–3m)
- ☀ **Aspect** Full sun
- ◉ **Soil type** Fertile, moist, well drained
- ◎ **Harvest** Midsummer—mid-fall

Which to choose

In addition to being suitable for cooking or eating raw, plums are also divided into gages, damsons, and bullaces, and each type has its own qualities.

Damsons are smaller than plums. With a sharper taste, they are best eaten cooked. Varieties include 'Merryweather' (*above*). Damsons have a dark skin.

Gages have a rich, sweet flavor, and can be eaten raw or cooked. The skin is green or yellow in color. Varieties include 'Old Green Gage' (*above*).

Bullaces are smaller than damsons, with a yellow or purple skin. They can be eaten raw when very ripe. Varieties include 'Langley Bullace' (*above*).

Eggplant 'Black Enorma'

Eggplants

A taste of the Mediterranean, these plump and glossy beauties need plenty of heat and sunlight to do well, so are best grown in a greenhouse or on a sunny, sheltered patio. Large, purple varieties are the most familiar, although eggplant comes in various colors, shapes, and sizes. Grow them from seed sown under cover in spring or buy young plants. Plant them into large containers or grow bags, and provide support. Pinch out their tips when they reach 12in (30cm) in length to encourage branching. Water regularly and feed every two weeks after the first flowers appear. Harvest the eggplants when they are shiny and firm, before the skin turns cloudy.

Highly perishable
A member of the nightshade family, the eggplant is related to peppers and tomatoes, and all prefer similar growing conditions. An eggplant is thought of as a vegetable but it is actually a berry. It becomes bitter with age and is highly perishable, which is another reason to grow your own, because nothing is fresher than when it is picked straight off of the vine.

AT A GLANCE
- **Plant type** Annual
- **Aspect** Full sun
- **Soil type** Fertile and moist
- **Sow seed** Early spring—mid-spring
- **Harvest** Late summer—mid-fall

Which to choose

There are various eggplant varieties to try that can all be grown in the same way. Consider growing more than one variety to enjoy a mixture of eggplant types.

White eggplants clearly gave rise to their name. Plants and seeds are not widely sold but varieties available include 'Snowy', 'Casper', and 'Easter Egg'.

Striped varieties taste the same as white or purple types, but add interest to cooked dishes. Varieties include 'Listade de Gandia' (*above*).

Penstemon 'Countess of Dalkeith'

Penstemons

These elegant, upright perennials bloom from summer to fall, bearing spikes of tubular flowers in a wide variety of cool or vibrant shades, from electric blue to deep scarlet. The boldest plants are the taller varieties, which are ideal for borders and containers, while compact forms make a good display in rockeries. For a prolonged show, deadhead regularly, stake taller plants, and water during dry spells. Not all penstemons are hardy, but new plants can easily be grown from cuttings (*see pp.194–195*). If kept under cover during winter, the cuttings will flower the following summer. In colder areas, mulch around plants growing outside to protect their roots.

A plant for water conservation

A native flower of North America, hardy types of penstemons have recently found a role in "xeriscaping," a sustainable method of landscape gardening that reduces or avoids the use of supplemental watering. For this type of gardening, choose penstemons native to the desert or alpine zones. These extremely hardy plants are ideal for sustainable landscaping, or for growing in areas with prolonged drought or reduced availability of water.

AT A GLANCE
- ❦ **Plant type** Hardy/half hardy perennial
- ⚑ **Height** 18in–6ft (45cm–2m)
- ◣ **Spread** 12–20in (30–50cm)
- ☼ **Aspect** Full sun or partial shade
- ◉ **Soil type** Fertile and well drained

Which to choose

The best varieties for stunning border displays are those that grow to at least 2ft (60cm) tall. These include 'Countess of Dalkeith' (*right*).

'White Bedder' gives a cool display from midsummer to mid-fall. Plant it near darker varieties for maximum contrast impact.

'Pensham Czar' bears spikes of purple-blue flowers with contrasting white throats. It is a good choice for containers if fed regularly.

'Chester Scarlet' has slender crimson blooms and flowers freely, creating a spectacular show. It is a tall choice, reaching 3ft (1m) in height.

Lavandula angustifolia

Lavender

Richly scented, adored by bees, and free-flowering, this versatile evergreen shrub is equally at home in modern and traditional garden styles. It is native to the Mediterranean, and needs plenty of sunshine and well drained sandy or gravely soil to grow well, but it can be short-lived. Use it as an informal hedge or to line a path, or plant it *en masse* to create a stunning display of color and to concentrate the fragrance. Compact forms are also ideal for containers and can be used to bring scent nearer the house. Lavender, or *Lavandula*, tolerates drought and requires little care or feeding after planting. Simply give it a light prune after flowering to maintain it (*see p.201*).

Sunshine and dry conditions

Good air circulation is important for growing healthy lavender plants. In areas of high humidity, fungus infection can cause root rot. Applying a mulch of crushed rocks, and not organic material that traps moisture around the base of the plant, avoids this problem.

AT A GLANCE
- ❧ **Plant type** Evergreen shrub
- ❦ **Height** 2–3ft (60–100cm)
- ❦ **Spread** 2–5ft (60cm–1.5m)
- ☼ **Aspect** Full sun
- ◉ **Soil type** Well drained

Which to choose

English lavender, *L. angustifolia*, is the most widely grown, but there are other species. These are equally attractive but need winter protection.

French lavender, *L. stoechas*, is a knee-high shrub with flaglike "bracts" on top of its flowers. Short-lived, treat it as bedding.

Mound-forming *L. dentata* bears pale purple flowers from midsummer until late summer. Its height and spread is 3 x 5ft (1 x 1.5m).

Ferny leaved *L. pinnata* produces tridentlike spikes of purple-blue flowers on long stems. It grows to 3ft (1m) in height and spread.

Perennial plants for
Cut flowers

Picking homegrown flowers for the house is a gardener's perk, and many perennials look as attractive in a vase as they do in the garden. Cutting flowers does encourage most perennials to produce more blooms, but don't pick so many that you spoil the display outside. To help them last, cut the flowers in the morning.

1 *Rudbeckia laciniata* This plant has long-lasting yellow flowers. 'Goldquelle' (*left*) has double blooms.
🌱 3ft (1m) ◣ 2ft (60cm)

2 *Helenium autumnale* The flowers of this late-summer perennial last for a week in water.
🌱 3ft (1m) ◣ 2ft (60cm)

3 *Leucanthemum* x *superbum* These simple white daisies look stunning planted in drifts in the garden, or arranged in a vase indoors.
🌱 36in (90cm) ◣ 20in (50cm)

4 *Dianthus caryophyllus* Unlike carnations bought at a florist's, garden blooms are richly scented.
🌱 20in (50cm) ◣ 8in (20cm)

5 *Alstroemeria aurea* Peruvian lilies bring a touch of the exotic to a garden border and can last up to three weeks as cut flowers.
🌱 3ft (1m) ◣ 18in (45cm)

6 *Phlox paniculata* Loved by bees, this tall favorite of the cottage garden and herbaceous border fills a room with delicious scent.
🌱 3ft (1m) ◣ 2ft (60cm)

7 *Liatris spicata* Flowering in late summer, it bears tall spikes of pink, mauve, or white blooms.
🌱 5ft (1.5m) ◣ 18in (45cm)

8 *Paeonia lactiflora* Peonies can be short-lived in a vase but it's a great way to enjoy their exquisite pink, white, or red blooms indoors.
🌱 20in (50cm) ◣ 28in (70cm)

9 *Crocosmia* x *crocosmiiflora* These fiery beauties look good planted in swathes in the garden, and can last two weeks in a vase.
🌱 24in (60cm) ◣ 6in (15cm)

10 *Astrantia major* Bees love the unusual-looking flowers of this cottage-garden plant. The flowers last well in water after cutting.
🌱 28in (70cm) ◣ 18in (45cm)

Chilie 'Hot Mexican'

Chilies

Attractive and highly productive, chilies are easy to grow and are ideal for pots. Warmth and sunlight bring on the largest crops, so they are best grown in a greenhouse or on a sunny windowsill or patio. Chilies vary greatly in size, shape, color, and heat, and there are hundreds of varieties to choose from. Sow seeds under cover in early spring or buy young plants, and grow them in containers or grow bags with support. Pinch out the young plants when 12in (30cm) tall to encourage bushiness, water regularly, and feed with tomato fertilizer every two weeks after the first flowers appear. Pick the first few chilies while they are still green to encourage more to form.

Warm the soil for a head start

To plant chilies in the ground, find out where your vegetable patch catches the most sun. In spring, warm up the soil with a black plastic cover. Once the soil is warm and the last frost has passed, plant seedlings in their final position 45cm (18in) apart.

AT A GLANCE
- ✹ **Plant type** Annual
- ☀ **Aspect** Full sun
- ◉ **Soil type** Compost or grow bags
- ⌄ **Sow seed** Early spring—mid-spring
- ◎ **Harvest** Late summer—mid-fall

Which to choose

Heat is an important factor when deciding which chili to grow—you do need to be able to eat them. And bear in mind that mild to one person could be hot to another.

Jalapeño is a type of chili, rather than a variety, and has a moderate to hot flavor. The chilies reach 1½in (4cm) long, and are harvested while green.

'Hungarian Hot Wax' is a mild-tasting variety that also crops well in cooler climates. The green chilies are the mildest, but even red ones are not hot.

'Cherry Bomb' is a prolific variety that produces small rounded chilies measuring 2in (5cm) across. These chilies have a moderate to hot flavor.

Blueberry 'Spartan'

Blueberries

Sumptuously sweet and rich in taste, these berries are easy to grow. The plants also make an attractive feature, with their white spring blossom and tinted fall foliage. Most are self-fertile, meaning you only need one plant to produce a crop, although growing two or more varieties to cross-pollinate each other produces a larger harvest. Keep them well watered and protect the fruit from birds, which will pillage the ripening berries.

Growing advice

Blueberries are acid-loving, so unless you have acid soil, you must grow blueberries in pots. Choose one at least 18in (45cm) across and fill it with acid soil mix.

Container-grown plants should be kept well watered at all times. Fertilize plants every 14 days starting from late spring until midsummer with acid fertilizer.

AT A GLANCE
- ❧ **Plant type** Hardy shrub
- ⚘ **Height** 3–6ft (1–2m)
- ◣ **Spread** 3–5ft (1–1.5m)
- ☀ **Aspect** Full sun or partial shade
- ◉ **Soil type** Acid, moist, well drained
- ◎ **Harvest** Midsummer—early fall

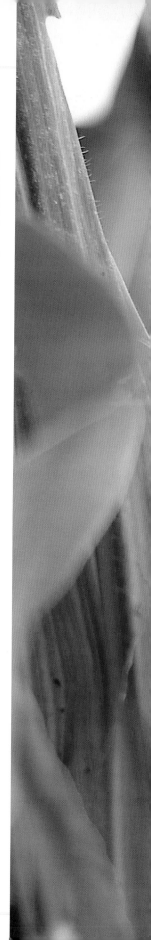

Corn 'Sundance'

Corn

Freshly harvested homegrown corn will always be sweeter and more tender than any you can buy, because its quality declines within hours of picking. Each of these simple-to-grow plants will produce one or two cobs, so plant the number you need accordingly. Seed is best sown under cover in small pots in spring (*see pp.72–73*), to plant outside when the risk of frost has passed. Wind spreads corn pollen, so plant it in blocks, not long rows, to assist pollination. Keep plants well watered during summer. Harvest the cobs once the tassels turn brown, but check for ripeness first (*see p.199*).

Pollinating by hand

Hand pollination is necessary where bee populations are in decline or, in the case of corn, if it has not been very windy. Male flowers bears stamens and contain pollen, and female flowers have stigma. Transferring pollen onto the female stigma using a small paintbrush or a cotton swab pollinates the female, enabling the fruit or vegetable to develop to full size. In the case of corn, you can assist pollination simply by shaking the flower tassels when they begin to open.

Growing advice

With its tall, upright habit, corn must be planted 18in (45cm) apart in blocks so the pollen from the male flowers falls easily into the female flowers.

When planting, use a marked stake or narrow plank of wood to help ensure plants are at the correct distance apart and spaced evenly.

Harvest the cobs as soon as they are ready to eat by twisting them off at the base. The cobs keep better with their outer leaves left intact.

AT A GLANCE
- ❧ **Plant type** Annual
- ☀ **Aspect** Full sun in shelter
- ◉ **Soil type** Fertile and well drained
- ↧ **Sow seed** Mid-spring—late-spring
- ◎ **Harvest** Late summer—early fall

Agapanthus 'Grand Design'

African lilies

Bearing large heads of trumpet blooms, these perennials, named *Agapanthus*, provide a vibrant display in rich shades of blue or white. They originate from southern Africa, and need plenty of sun and moisture to grow well. There are many varieties to choose from but only deciduous forms that die back in winter are reliably hardy; evergreen plants should be brought inside for winter. Ideal for the front of a border, they can also be grown in containers if repotted every 2–3 years. Feed regularly throughout summer for the best display.

Planting partners

African lilies flower over a long period and combine well with many other sun-loving plants. Plant them alongside those with contrasting flower colors.

Sea holly, *Eryngium*, flowers at a similar time to African lilies, with white or blue blooms. The heads dry *in situ* and last into winter.

Cotton lavender, *Santolina*, is a shrubby plant with gray-green leaves and yellow flowers. Use it as a backdrop to African lilies.

AT A GLANCE

- **Plant type** Hardy/tender perennial
- **Height** 2–6ft (60cm–2m)
- **Spread** 1–2ft (30–60cm)
- **Aspect** Full sun
- **Soil type** Fertile, moist, well drained

Pepper 'Redskin'

Peppers

Also known as sweet peppers or bell peppers, these are very tasty and come in a range of colors, shapes, and sizes. The plants need warmth and sunlight to crop well, so are best grown in a greenhouse or outside in a sunny location. They are also suitable for containers. Grow peppers from seed sown under cover in spring, or buy young plants. Insert stakes to support large peppers and keep plants well watered. As soon as flowers appear, apply tomato fertilizer every 14 days. Pick when big enough to use, whether green, yellow, or red.

Growing advice

Peppers have tough stalks that are best cut using pruning shears when harvesting. Pulling a pepper off by hand can damage the plant's stems.

AT A GLANCE
- ❀ **Plant type** Annual
- ☀ **Aspect** Full sun
- ◉ **Soil type** Fertile and moist
- ⋁ **Sow seed** Early spring—mid-spring
- ◎ **Harvest** Late summer—early fall

Jobs to do:
Summer

Around the yard:
- Plant bedding displays.
- Mow lawns, and trim hedges and topiary regularly.
- Remove excess weed from ponds.

In the vegetable garden:
- Net fruit crops against birds.
- Harvest crops as they mature.
- Hill the soil up around potatoes as they grow.

In beds and borders:
- Water plants during dry spells.
- Deadhead flowering plants.
- Take cuttings from shrubs.

Early summer

Summer brings warmer weather and longer days, encouraging all crops and ornamental plants to grow rapidly. Keeping them well watered is essential now, especially for early crops that are soon ready to harvest. Devise a weekly routine to help you keep on top of tasks at this time.

Essential jobs:

* Plant summer bedding plants into position (*see p.185*).
* Plant vegetable seedlings sown directly in seed beds (*see p.186*).
* Train cordon tomatoes and remove sideshoots (*see p.186*).
* Protect fruiting crops from birds using nets (*see p.187*).
* Cut back spring-flowering bulbs as they die back (*see p.188*).
* Remove the growing tips from broad beans (*see p.188*).
* Harvest crops regularly for a continued supply (*see p.189*).
* Feed fruiting crops with high-potash fertilizer (*see p.190*).
* Remove excess weed and algae from ponds (*see p.191*).

Last chance to:

* Sow hardy seeds directly outside (*see pp.70–71*).
* Lift and divide spring-flowering bulbs (*see p.261*).
* Harvest asparagus; now leave the stems in place to grow all summer.

Continue to:

* Stake perennials and taller bulbs as they grow (*see p.72*).
* Tie climbing crops and ornamentals to their supports.
* Mow the lawn regularly and remove the clippings.
* Trim evergreen shrubs to keep them tidy (*see p.83*).
* Add leafy and twiggy material to the compost pile.

Watch out for:

* Birds feeding on brassica crops and soft fruit—protect plants and fruits using nets.

Crops to sow:

Outside: Beets, calabrese, carrots, zucchini, Florence fennel, green and string beans, kale, kohlrabi, lettuces, peas, pumpkins, radishes, spinach, spring cabbages, sprouting broccoli, squashes, summer cauliflowers, rutabagas, Swiss chard, and turnips.
Under cover: Cucumbers

Crops to plant:

Eggplants, Brussels sprouts, celery root, celery, chilies, zucchini, cucumbers, green and string beans, kale, leeks, peppers, sprouting broccoli, and summer cauliflowers.

Harvest now:

Asparagus, beets, broad beans, calabrese, carrots, cherries, currants, early potatoes, Florence fennel, garlic, globe artichokes, gooseberries, kohlrabi, lettuces, peas, radishes, rhubarb, spinach, spring cabbages, Swiss chard, strawberries, and turnips.

Plant summer bedding displays

Once the risk of frost has passed it's safe to plant bedding plants that have been hardened off (*see p.77*) into beds, containers, and hanging baskets. Add some slow-release fertilizer as you plant to help prolong the display, and protect the plants from slug and snail damage.

Training tomatoes into cordons—a single stem grown up a support—is started when the plants are young. Tie the main stem to a vertical support, such as a stake or string, and remove any sideshoots that develop in the leaf joints. Pinching these out stops the plants from wasting energy on unwanted growth and encourages a larger crop.

Lightly trimming shrubby herbs, such as rosemary, sage, bay, and thyme improves their shape, and encourages them to bush out and produce flavorsome new growth. Prune rosemary and thyme after flowering but remove the flower buds from sage. If growing bay as topiary, shape it now.

Vegetable plants raised in seed beds, such as summer cabbages and leeks, can now be lifted and planted into their final position in the vegetable garden. Dig them up carefully to avoid damaging the roots, and water well after planting. Check the seed package for the correct spacings between plants and rows.

Trim hedges and topiary now and at regular intervals throughout the summer, first making sure that any nesting birds have left before you start. Clip off excess new growth and neaten the hedge or topiary on all sides. Avoid cutting into older growth, especially when trimming conifers, which may not grow back, leaving bald patches behind.

Citrus plants protected under cover during winter can now be moved outside for summer. Harden them off first (*see p. 77*) to acclimatize them to life outdoors, then locate them a sunny, sheltered spot. Water regularly and feed the plants using a special citrus plant fertilizer, which is available from larger garden centers, nurseries, or online.

Cover fruit bushes and trees with nets to deter birds. This is best done before the fruit starts to ripen, when it is then easy to spot. Pull the netting taut to prevent birds from getting snagged in it, and pin it down securely at soil level, otherwise birds will sneak underneath. If you have several plants, erect a simple cage using stakes and nets. Trees are harder to protect, but cover what you can with nets or horticultural fleece.

Spring-flowering bulbs can be cut to the base once their leaves have yellowed and died. All but tulips can be left undisturbed to flower again next year. Tulips rarely flower reliably for a second year if left in the soil, and should be lifted, dried, and stored. They can then be replanted late in the fall.

Continue providing support for taller perennials and bulbs as they grow to prevent them from collapsing. This is most necessary for those with slender stems, such as penstemons, or large flowers, like lilies. Insert individual garden stakes for single stems or use several for clump-forming perennial plants.

Remove the tops from broad bean plants once the first bean pods begin to form, pinching off the top 3in (7cm) of growth. This will encourage an earlier harvest by stopping leafy growth. It also helps to deter blackflies, which commonly infest the soft growing tips, weakening the plants by sucking their sap.

Regular harvests

Harvesting vegetable crops as soon as they are ready allows you to enjoy them at their freshest and best. It also encourages those that crop over a long period, such as beans and peas, to produce larger harvests. Other vegetables that are harvested whole, such as carrots and radishes, can be resown quickly to harvest again a few weeks later.

Shading and ventilating your greenhouse will stop it from overheating and drying out in sunny spells, which can damage plants. Open the doors and vents, and install shading material or apply shade paint to the glass. Soak the floor regularly to increase humidity levels.

Applying high-potash fertilizer

1 Tomato fertilizer is rich in potash, which encourages plants to flower and produce fruit. Apply it weekly to all fruiting crops, such as tomatoes, peppers, eggplants, and zucchini once their first flowers have appeared.

2 Prepare the tomato fertilizer as directed on the package and apply it directly to the roots. Avoid splashing the leaves, especially on sunny days, because the feed can damage them.

Enjoy free new strawberry plants by using pieces of bent wire to peg the "runners" (see p.85) to the soil or the surface of a compost-filled pot buried in the soil. Keep them well watered. Let them produce roots and keep growing until late summer. Cut the new plant from its parent, and plant it in the soil.

Removing algae and floating weeds from ponds helps to keep them healthy by allowing sunlight to reach the water. Use a net to scoop off excess weeds, and a stake to tease out the algae. Planting aquatic plants (*see pp. 126–127*) also helps keep the water clear.

Variegated plants often produce vigorous, plain green shoots, which is known as "reversion." If left to grow, these shoots can take over from the slower-growing colored growth, spoiling the appearance of your plant. Check variegated plants occasionally and prune out any green stems while young.

Time to prune Shrubs and fruit bushes are pruned now to promote flowers and cropping.

Late spring-flowering shrubs and trees, such as philadelphus and evergreen ceanothus, are pruned after flowering. Cut back flowered shoots to healthy buds, remove any weak growth, and trim back excessively long shoots. On mature plants, very old and woody stems that no longer flower can be cut to the base.

Fruiting currants and gooseberries are pruned now. To prune black currants, remove some of the oldest stems to the base to let light into the center. Remove any dead or weak growth as well. This can also be done in winter. To prune the other currants and gooseberries, cut new sideshoots back to five leaves each. Shorten these again in winter to one bud, and prune one-quarter of the oldest stems to the base, plus any weak or crossing growth.

Midsummer

As summer comes to its peak, many fruit and vegetable crops will be ready to harvest, and ornamental borders will be in full bloom. Watering well, picking produce while fresh, and deadheading spent flowers are all important now to make the most of your earlier hard work.

Essential jobs:

* Thin fruit trees to ensure full-sized fruit (*see p.193*).
* Dry onions, shallots, and garlic on racks (*see p.194*).
* Provide drinking water for garden wildlife (*see p.194*).
* Stop cordon tomatoes by removing the tops (*see p.195*).
* Mulch thirsty crops to help retain moisture (*see p.196*).
* Remove suckers (*see p.196*).
* Cut back excessive new growth on shrubs (*see p.197*).
* Summer-prune established wisteria plants (*see p.197*).
* Prune group 2 clematis after flowering (*see p.197*).
* Prune established cherry and plum trees (*see p.197*).

Last chance to:

* Sow quick-growing crops outside in the soil to harvest before fall (*see pp.70–71*).

Continue to:

* Weed beds and borders.
* Mow the lawn regularly and keep hedges and topiary trimmed.
* Harvest all crops as soon as they are ready to pick.
* Water all crops regularly during dry spells.
* Cut back flowered perennials for a second flush of color.
* Water and feed container and basket displays regularly.
* Deadhead flowering plants for a long-lasting display.

Watch out for:

* Blight on tomato plants—treat with fungicide and discard affected fruit.

Crops to sow:

Outside: Beets, calabrese, carrots, Florence fennel, green and string beans, kale, kohlrabi, lettuces, radishes, spinach, spring cabbages, and turnips.

Crops to plant:

Chilies, zucchini, green and string beans, kale, leeks, maincrop potatoes, peppers, sprouting broccoli, squashes, summer cauliflowers, and winter cabbages and cauliflowers.

Harvest now:

Beets, broad beans, calabrese, carrots, cherries, zucchini, cucumbers, currants, early potatoes, Florence fennel, green and string beans, garlic, gooseberries, kohlrabi, lettuces, onions and shallots, peas, radishes, rhubarb, spinach, spring cabbages, strawberries, summer cauliflowers, summer raspberries, summer squashes, Swiss chard, tomatoes, and turnips.

Thinning fruits

Fruit trees, such as apples, pears, and plums often produce masses of fruitlets, which, if allowed to remain, would result in undersized and unhealthy fruit. Some young fruit naturally falls at this point, known as "June drop," but you may still need to thin them further. Thin the remaining fruits to about 4in (10cm) apart. To prevent pests and diseases from developing, put healthy fruits that fall, as well as those you have thinned out, in the compost pile.

Onion, shallot, and garlic plants will soon turn yellow and collapse, meaning the bulbs are ready to harvest. At this point, lift the bulbs and place them on wire racks to dry. Keep them outside if the weather is dry. If not, store them under cover in a dry, airy place, such as in a shed.

Keeping birdbaths filled during summer is a sure way to attract birds and other wildlife into your garden. Birds and animals can struggle to find enough to drink during hot, dry periods, and birds in particular like to bathe regularly to keep cool. If you can, place your birdbath in the shade so the water evaporates less quickly. Raise it off of the ground, too, to deter stalking cats.

Growing plants from semi-ripe wood cuttings

2 Trim each shoot so that they are around 3–4in (8–10cm) in length, or slightly longer if the plant has large leaves. Remove the main growing tip and trim the base of the stem just below a leaf joint. Nip off the lowest leaves, creating some bare stem to ease into the compost, aiming to leave 4–6 leaves per cutting.

1 Semi-ripe cuttings are so-called because the base of the cutting is woody while the tip is soft. Early in the day when they are full of sap, cut off some healthy, nonflowering shoots. Place them in a plastic bag filled with a little water to keep them fresh while you collect more cutting material.

Removing faded flowers from plants, or "deadheading," keeps them tidy and encourages them to produce new blooms. Pinch off individual flowers with your fingers and cut spent flowerheads back to a bud or a leaf. Leave any plants that have attractive seedheads in fall.

Cordon tomatoes should be "stopped" once they have formed four or five trusses of fruits, or have reached the top of their support. This means removing the top of the main stem to two leaves above the uppermost flower truss. This stops the plant from wasting energy on unwanted growth and instead diverts it to producing bigger fruit.

To stop cauliflower heads from discoloring loosely tie some of the plant's own leaves over it to exclude the light. Do this on a dry day to avoid trapping moisture that could rot the head, or "curd," and try not to splash the plant when watering it. Occasionally open the leaves up to check for pests and to allow the head dry out after rain.

3 Dip the bare base of the cutting into hormone rooting powder, making sure that the cut is properly covered. This should help it to root more quickly. Gently tap the cutting to shake off any excess powder.

4 Insert the cuttings into a pot of moist soil mix, cover with a clear plastic bag, and position in a cool, light spot, away from direct sun. Keep the soil mix moist and the cuttings should have rooted by fall—pull them very gently to check.

Mulching thirsty vegetable crops, such as peas, beans, and zucchini, helps to retain moisture in the soil and reduces how frequently you need to water them—saving you time. Water plants thoroughly first, then apply a thick layer of well rotted garden compost or manure near their base but not touching the stems. The mulch will also help to suppress emerging weeds.

Many trees and shrubs produce suckers from their base and, if left unchecked, these unwanted, fast-growing shoots will turn into poor-quality new plants of little garden use. Use pruners to tear them off (don't cut them) from as close to the base as possible. This will help to ensure they don't resprout.

Fruit attracts wasps that can spoil a crop by eating holes into them, and may sting you if they are disturbed. Avoid this by hanging wasp traps in your fruit trees. These are made by filling jars with sugary liquid and adding a lid with a small hole pierced through it. The wasps are lured in by the liquid but then can't escape.

Removing yellowing leaves from pond plants before they sink or fall into the water helps to keep the pond clean and healthy. Carefully work from the edge of the pond or lay a ladder or platform across the water, ensuring it is secure.

Excessively long new shoots on shrubs can spoil the overall appearance of the plant. Prune them back in line with other new shoots surrounding it so that the plant maintains a good shape. Rose bushes commonly produce long new stems in summer, known as "water shoots." Cut them back hard to a healthy bud.

Time to prune *Many shrubs, climbers, and fruit bushes can be pruned for shape and flowers.*

Early summer-flowering shrubs, such as rock roses and weigela, should now be pruned. Cut flowered stems back to healthy buds, remove any dead, damaged, or diseased growth, and prune any very old and woody branches down to the base.

Wisterias are pruned in summer and winter (*see p.302*). Prune now by cutting back all the wiry new stems so that they have 5–7 pairs of leaves each. This controls the size of the plant, which can be large, and promotes the formation of flower buds for spring.

Group 2 clematis, such as 'Nelly Moser', that have finished flowering for the first time can be cut back. Prune back some of the shoots that bloomed to healthy buds, which will encourage a second flush of flowers. Prune again in winter (*see p.309*).

Plums, cherries, and apricots are lightly pruned, and only in summer, to avoid a serious disease called *silver leaf*. Simply remove any dead, dying, or diseased branches, and any that are crossing or rubbing. Aim to create a goblet-shaped tree with an airy, open heart.

Late summer

The season for many plants is beginning to close, and while your borders may be starting to look tired, the vegetable patch will be bountiful as your crops mature. Harvest fruits and vegetables as soon as they are ready, and deadhead flowering plants regularly to prolong their display.

Essential jobs:
* Check corn for ripeness before harvesting (*see p.199*).
* Collect seeds from annuals and perennials (*see p.200*).
* Cut back this year's growth on lavender bushes (*see p.201*).
* Clean the filter pads inside of pond pumps (*see p.201*).
* Prune back and tie in summer raspberries after fruiting (*see p.201*).
* Take semi-ripe cuttings of tender perennials (*see p.201*).
* Remove any fallen leaves and plant debris from the surface of ponds.
* Clear away any old growth and debris as plants and crops die back.
* Order spring-flowering bulbs to plant during fall.

Last chance to:
* Prune the new summer growth on wisterias (*see p.197*).

Continue to:
* Weed beds and borders regularly, including the vegetable patch.
* Mow the lawn regularly.
* Provide water for birds and garden wildlife (*see p.194*).
* Lift and dry late onions, shallots, and garlic bulbs (*see p.194*).
* Water all crops regularly.
* Water and feed container and basket displays regularly.
* Deadhead flowering plants for a long-lasting display.
* Tie in new growth on climbers and wall shrubs.

Crops to sow:
Outside: Carrots, kohlrabi, lettuces, spinach, spring cabbages, Swiss chard, and turnips.

Crops to plant:
Sprouting broccoli and strawberries.

Harvest now:
Eggplants, beets, blackberries, blueberries, calabrese, carrots, celery, cherries, chilies, zucchini, cucumbers, currants, early potatoes, Florence fennel, green and string beans, garlic, kohlrabi, lettuces, onions and shallots, peas, peppers, plums, radishes, spinach, squashes, strawberries, summer- and fall-fruiting raspberries, summer cabbages and cauliflowers, corn, Swiss chard, tomatoes, and turnips.

Watch out for:
* Wasps around fruit crops—hang traps near your plants and in fruit trees (*see p.196*).

Ripe corn A cob of corn is ready to harvest when its silky tassels have turned brown. To be doubly sure, carefully tease open the cob and pierce a kernel with your thumbnail. The sap that comes out should look creamy. Harvest by twisting the cob from the plant, and eat as soon as possible for maximum tenderness and sweetness.

Collect seeds

For free plants next year, collect seeds from seedheads and pods from around the garden now. Choose a dry day and gently crush the seedheads or pods to free the seeds, then place them into labeled envelopes. Store them in a cool, dry place, ready to sow next year.

Trimming lavender bushes as the flowers fade ensures that the shrubs keep a good shape and don't become leggy with lots of old, woody growth. Remove the flowered stalks and about 1in (2½cm) of green growth below that. Avoid cutting back into older, woodier stems as they often don't resprout.

Pond pump filters can become blocked with algae, plant debris, and silt, which prevents them from working properly. Cleaning them regularly helps to keep pond water clear and healthy for plants and fish. It also ensures water features work as they should. Replace any damaged or missing filters.

Time to prune Pruning summer raspberry plants now encourages fruiting stems for next year.

Summer raspberries can be pruned once all the fruit has been harvested. Cut the fruited canes down to ground level, then tie in 6–8 of the new nonfruiting stems per plant along their supports. Prune any surplus new stems down to the base.

Taking cuttings of tender perennials, such as penstemon, fuchsias, and geraniums, allows you to keep the young plants under cover and safe from frost, in case the parent plant dies. Look for nonflowering shoots and take semi-ripe wood cuttings (*see pp.194–195*). Plant them outside in late spring.

Fall

Signs of Fall

It's the season of mellow fruitfulness when fruits ripen and vegetables are harvested. Many annuals and perennials will flower until the first frosts, but the garden is winding down. Annuals are setting seed, perennials are dying back, and deciduous trees and shrubs are losing their leaves, but not before they've put on a spectacularly colorful show.

Fall equinox

The fall equinox occurs around September 22–23, marking the point at which the Northern Hemisphere begins to tilt away from the Sun, and signaling the beginning of fall. At this time, the length of the day and night are roughly the same, just as with the vernal equinox in spring (*see p.17*).

Day length

As the Northern Hemisphere continues to tilt away from the Sun, so the number of daylight hours received gradually decreases each day until the winter solstice (*see p.277*). This is most pronounced in the north, where the sun rises later and sets earlier than in the south. In Alaska, for example, there can be fewer than six hours of daylight on the shortest days.

Weather

In fall, some parts of the US can experience a warm, dry period with temperatures above 70°F (21°C), which follows a period of cool weather. Known as an "Indian summer," it is an interlude of warm, dry weather before the next season sets in, whether it is a cold and snowy season or an extended rainy one, depending on location. In addition, fall can often bring unsettled weather, storms, and cold snaps, so it is a good time to check that plants are well supported and properly protected in preparation for wilder weather ahead.

Temperature

The season averages for daytime temperatures are 54 °F (12°C), falling as the season progresses. While the days can be relatively mild, frost becomes more common at night, and it can kill or damage tender plants. "Ground frost" occurs at soil level and is less damaging to plants than "air frost," when the air around the plants is below freezing point. Frost is more likely farther north, so if you live in southern, southeastern or western states your garden is less likely to be affected. Many thermometers and weather stations come with a frost alert. Alternatively, check your local forecast.

Plant science

Fall is an important season for plants as they ripen their fruits, disperse seeds, and prepare themselves for winter or, in the case of annuals, die. It is a time of complex and colorful chemistry and biology.

ANNUALS

Even when regularly deadheaded, (*see p.91*) all summer annuals, which includes many vegetable crops, start dying off at this time of year. Exactly what triggers this isn't fully known, but it could be related to physical exhaustion, a lack of life-sustaining new growth, plant hormones, or a response to the shortening days. Leaves turn yellow and drop off, and stems and roots die back until the plant is completely dead. It lives on through the seeds it produced in summer (unless deadheaded), which, in some species, can be several thousand.

When annual plants set enough seeds their flowering ceases.

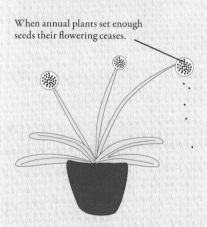

Annual plants die completely and their nutrients are absorbed by the soil.

Passage of nutrients into soil.

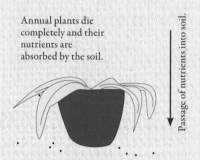

PERENNIALS

Once flowering finishes, the leafy top growth turns yellow as the valuable nutrients and sugars it contains are drawn into the roots, and converted to starch for storage. The stored starch sustains the plant, which may continue to produce new roots, even though dormant. The shortening days also prompt the development of new shoots and flower buds at the base of the plant, ready to grow in spring. These can occur above or below the soil. If the plant is slightly tender, it will need frost protection using a garden-compost mulch or a frost blanket.

All top growth dies back, often changing color as it does so.

Passage of nutrients into the roots.

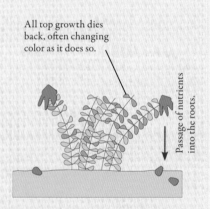

Nutrients are stored in the roots, which may continue to grow.

TREES AND SHRUBS

Fall triggers chlorophyll, the green pigment in plant leaves, to break down in deciduous species, leaving red and orange pigments that create the fiery tints of fall. The leaves drop off when ethylene, a gas, builds up inside, causing cells in the stalks to die, letting them detach without leaving a wound. Nutrients are drawn deeper into plant tissues, and new growth toughens as cells are reinforced with a chemical called lignin. As fruits mature, bitter-tasting tannins are converted to sugars and their tissues soften to attract dispersing animals and birds.

Leaves change color as their green pigment breaks down.

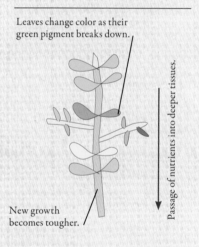

New growth becomes tougher.

Passage of nutrients into deeper tissues.

Fruit tissues soften and sweeten to encourage seed dispersal.

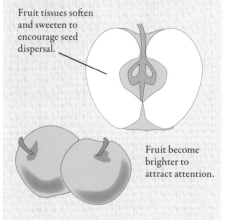

Fruit become brighter to attract attention.

Anemone x *hybrida* 'Hadspen Abundance'

Japanese anemones

With their large simple flowers and wiry stems, these reliable perennials make an elegant addition to the fall border. Flowering in shades of pink and white, they are ideal for bringing color to cooler, shadier corners of the garden. They prefer soil rich in organic matter so, using a garden fork, dig in well rotted garden compost when planting. Stake taller varieties for support and deadhead spent flowers. Divide oversized clumps (*see p.261*).

Which to choose

The most widely available fall-flowering Japanese anemones are varieties of *A. hupehensis*, such as 'Hadspen Abundance' (*right*), which grow to 2–3ft (60–90cm) in height, and those of *A.* x *hybrida*, including 'Honorine Jobert' (*below*), which can reach 4–5ft (1.2–1.5m) tall. All are reliable and easy to grow.

AT A GLANCE
- ❧ **Plant type** Hardy perennial
- ⚘ **Height** 2–5ft (60cm–1.5m)
- ◣ **Spread** 16in (40cm)–indefinite
- ☀ **Aspect** Full sun or dappled shade
- ◉ **Soil type** Fertile and moist

Apple 'Jonagold'
(dessert)

Apples

Apples are one of the most rewarding
fruit trees to grow and there are varieties
to serve all purposes, from sweet dessert
apples to eat raw, to sharper types for
cooking. Whatever variety you choose,
they are all available grafted onto a
range of rootstocks that control their
vigor and size. That means there are trees
suitable for any size of plot, or even
containers. New trees should be watered
regularly for their first year and mulched
annually in spring. Once established, apple
trees need only routine pruning in winter
to encourage healthy plant growth and
a bountiful harvest (*see p.305*).

AT A GLANCE
- **Plant type** Hardy deciduous tree
- **Height** 6–20ft (1.8–6m)
- **Spread** 6–15ft (1.8–5m)
- **Aspect** Full sun
- **Soil type** Fertile, moist, well drained
- **Harvest** Early fall—late fall

Choosing apples

In order to set fruit, apple flowers must be cross-pollinated with a compatible variety that blooms at the same time, known as a "pollinator." Unless there is one growing nearby, you may need to buy two trees to ensure a crop. Seek advice at the garden center for the best variety, rootstock, and pollinator.

Garden trees

Apples crop better when grown directly in the soil, and new trees are best planted while dormant (*see p.272*). Unless you have a lot of space, consider trees grafted onto dwarfing or semi-dwarfing rootstocks, which limit their mature height to 6–12ft (1.8–4m). If space is limited, consider buying a "family tree" that has two varieties grafted onto the same rootstock, which can eliminate the requirement for a second pollinator tree.

In containers

Apples grow happily in containers providing they are kept very well watered, especially when in fruit, and are mulched with garden compost each spring. The best trees for containers are less vigorous varieties grafted onto a semi-dwarfing rootstock, such as M26. Site container-grown trees in a sunny spot, away from strong winds, and repot them every 2–3 years (*see p.268*).

'Spartan'
(dessert)

'Discovery'
(dessert)

'Gravenstein' ....
(dessert)

'Cox's Orange
Pippin' (dessert)

'Howgate Wonder'
(cooking)

Dahlia 'Formby Perfection'

Dahlias

Flowering in an almost endless array of colors, shapes, and sizes, dahlias are simple and rewarding to grow. They range from compact varieties, ideal for pots, to large specimens that are best planted in borders. They begin flowering in summer, but their peak display comes in fall when they continue flowering freely until the first hard frost. Border dahlias are grown from half-hardy tubers planted in spring. In mild areas they can survive in the soil during winter, but elsewhere they must be lifted and brought under cover. Bedding dahlias are purchased as young plants or can be grown from seed. For the best display, deadhead or pick dahlias regularly, and support taller varieties with stakes.

AT A GLANCE
- ❦ **Plant type** Half hardy bulbs
- ⚑ **Height** 18in–5ft (45cm–1.5m)
- ◣ **Spread** 18–30in (45–75cm)
- ☀ **Aspect** Full sun, sheltered from wind
- ◉ **Soil type** Fertile and well drained

Choosing dahlias

Dahlias are highly varied, with flowers ranging from 4–10in (10–25cm) across, and have either green or deep bronze foliage. All enjoy the same growing conditions. However, large-flowered forms benefit from being grown in a sheltered site to prevent their impressive blooms from being damaged by bad weather.

D. 'Davenport Honey'

D. 'Glorie van Heemstede'

Dahlia 'Easter Sunday'

D. 'HS
First Love'

D. 'Alfred
Grille'

Growing advice

Dahlias are versatile, free-flowering plants, suitable
for both border and container displays. They are also
an excellent source for cut flowers for the home.

Border dahlias are upright, branching plants,
and all but the most compact need supporting.
These dahlias can be kept from year to year.

Compact bedding dahlias are usually treated
like annuals, and are discarded at the end of the
growing season. Buy fresh plants each spring.

Cut border dahlias regularly to ensure a constant
supply for indoors, but leave enough in the garden
for a good display. Bedding types can't be cut.

Sedum spectabile 'Brilliant'

Border sedums

These drought-tolerant perennials are invaluable for the front of a fall border, and flower in shades of pink and white. Their fleshy, succulent leaves are also attractive and vary in color from pale gray-green to rich glossy purple, giving interest earlier in the year. They lend themselves to many planting styles, and are magnets for bees and butterflies. Most have attractive seedheads, so don't cut them back in fall and they'll provide winter interest. Sedums do best on soils that aren't too fertile. They need good drainage and don't like wet or heavy soils. Tall varieties may splay out from the middle—cut them back in late spring to help prevent this.

Sustainable and drought-proof

If you are gardening with reduced water (*see p.166*), or you have limited time for watering in high summer, sedum, with its water-storing leaves, will provide your garden with a leafy, colorful display. Good drainage is essential, and avoid using organic mulch, which can retain too much moisture around the plant. Not only do pollinating insects visit sedums in summer, in winter, sedums attract birds.

AT A GLANCE
- **Plant type** Hardy perennial
- **Height** 12–24in (30–60cm)
- **Spread** 12–18in (30–45cm)
- **Aspect** Full sun
- **Soil type** Poor and well drained

Which to choose

Varieties of *Sedum spectabile* (*see left*) all have attractive gray-green foliage, but for even more color, consider those with rich purple or brightly variegated leaves.

S. erythrostictum 'Mediovariegatum' has boldly variegated foliage and produces clusters of pale pink flowers. It gives a long season of interest.

S. telephium Atropurpureum Group has dark stems and leaves that contrast with its paler flower buds. There are many named varieties to choose.

Chrysanthemum 'Imp'

Chrysanthemums

These tender perennials are highly varied, bearing flowers in a diverse range of shapes and colors. Most are tall, ideal for the back of borders, and are excellent for cutting. New plants are best bought each spring or grown from cuttings taken from plants brought inside for winter. Shortly after planting, pinch out the tips to encourage more flower shoots, and provide support for taller varieties. When frost kills the flowers, cut the stems back and protect the crown with thick mulch. In colder areas, lift the plants and move them to a cold frame or an unheated greenhouse until spring.

Which to choose

Double-flowered chrysanthemums, such as 'Membury' (*above*), are the most dramatic, and can be fully round or flattened in shape.

Single-flowered varieties, like 'Talbot Jo' (*above*), have simpler, weather-resistant blooms that are ideal for exposed plots.

AT A GLANCE
- ❧ **Plant type** Half hardy perennial
- ❦ **Height** 1–5ft (30cm–1.5m)
- ◭ **Spread** 2–3ft (60–100cm)
- ☀ **Aspect** Full sun
- ◉ **Soil type** Fertile and well drained

Aster amellus 'Blue King'

Autumn asters

Coming into bloom as other perennials are dying back, fall-flowering asters breathe new life into borders. Plant them in drifts in a mixture of varieties for an easy-to-grow medley of pink, blue, white, or purple daisy blooms. These upright branching plants are ideal for a mid-border position. Taller forms require staking, especially if grown in exposed sites. Deadhead plants regularly and water them well during dry periods to stop powdery mildew from developing on the leaves. Established clumps can be lifted and divided if congested to restore their vigor (*see p.261*).

A late but welcome garden feature

Asters can be planted any time after the final frost and will come into bloom in late summer and fall. Perennial asters, however, can be planted as late as fall, as long as they are kept watered until the soil freezes. A little mulch around the base of the plants will help retain moisture. Keep asters under control by pulling out the unwanted ones.

AT A GLANCE
- ⚘ **Plant type** Hardy perennial
- ⚑ **Height** 30in–5ft (75cm–1.5m)
- ⬟ **Spread** 18–36in (45–90cm)
- ☀ **Aspect** Full sun or light shade
- ◉ **Soil type** Moist but well drained

Which to choose

When selecting asters to grow for fall color, choose from varieties of *A. amellus*, *A. novae-angliae*, and *A. novi-belgii*.

Dome-forming *Aster amellus* (*left*) forms a spreading clump of color, ideal for the front of a border. *A. novae-angliae* (*above*) is taller with an upright habit; plant it mid-border.

Michaelmas daisy, *A. novi-belgii* (*above*), is similar to *A. novae-angliae*, and can be used in the same way in the garden. There are many varieties and colors to choose from.

Grasses for fall
Seedheads

Ornamental grasses are invaluable for adding structure, movement, and texture to a border, especially if planted *en masse*. At their peak in fall when their seedheads turn buff or silver, ornamental grasses often persist into winter.

1 *Cortaderia selloana* Evergreen pampas grass is a large plant, ideal for island beds and borders.
♠ 8ft (2.5m) ◣ 5ft (1.5m)

2 *Panicum virgatum* This bears billowing clouds of tiny flowers that sway gently in the wind.
♠ 5ft (1.5m) ◣ 3ft (1m)

3 *Miscanthus sinensis* Tall and clump-forming, this grass is ideal for summer screening, with colorful variegated forms to grow.
♠ 6ft (1.8m) ◣ 4ft (1.2m)

4 *Eragrostis curvula* Delicate and graceful, this large grass bears arching panicles of flowers.
♠ 4ft (1.2m) ◣ 4ft (1.2m)

5 *Lagurus ovatus* Known as hare's tails, this is a compact annual grass to grow from seed.
♠ 20in (50cm) ◣ 20in (50cm)

6 *Calamagrostis brachytricha* A large plant, it flowers in late summer and turns golden in fall.
♠ 4ft (1.2m) ◣ 3ft (1m)

7 *Chasmanthium latifolium* This broad-leaved grass has unusual diamond-shaped flowers that are excellent for drying.
♠ 3ft (1m) ◣ 2ft (60cm)

8 *Pennisetum setaceum* Known as fountain grass, it bears long, tactile blooms. Protect it in winter.
♠ 3ft (1m) ◣ 2ft (60cm)

9 *Briza maxima* Annual quaking grass has flowerheads that quiver in the breeze. It self-seeds readily.
♠ 20in (50cm) ◣ 12in (30cm)

10 *Stipa calamagrostis* This grass has narrow, arching leaves, topped by silvery flowerheads that turn beige during fall.
♠ 3ft (1m) ◣ 4ft (1.2m)

Pear 'Le Lectier'
(dessert)

Pears

Pears taste amazing when perfectly ripe
(*see below*) and growing your own is the
best way to enjoy them in peak condition.
They are grown in a similar way to apples
(*see pp.210–213*) but, because their early
blossom can be damaged by frost, pear
trees need a warmer, more sheltered site
There are many varieties to choose from,
either dessert or cooking types, available on
dwarfing and semi-dwarfing rootstocks. Like
apples, pear blossoms must be pollinated by
another variety to set fruit, so you may need
to plant more than one to obtain a crop. Water
new trees regularly in their first year, and
mulch established specimens with well rotted
garden compost in spring. Prune pear trees in
winter (*see p.305*).

Storing pears for ripening

While an apple can be picked fully ripe and
ready to eat, some pears need to be stored on
a rack in a basement or garage to give the hard
flesh time to soften. Harvest pears as soon as
they will detach from the tree. Summer pears
will be ready to eat before long but European
pears, the main type cultivated in North
America, may need up to a month in storage.

AT A GLANCE
- ꙮ **Plant type** Hardy deciduous tree
- ♠ **Height** 11–20ft (3.5–6m)
- ◤ **Spread** 10–12ft (3–4m)
- ☼ **Aspect** Full sun in shelter
- ◎ **Soil type** Fertile, moist, well drained
- ◎ **Harvest** Early fall—mid-fall

Which to choose

Some pears can be picked and eaten straight from the tree, but there are cooking varieties, such as 'Catillac'. As a compromise, consider dual-purpose pears that can be cooked or enjoyed raw.

'Williams' Bon Chrétien' is a dual-purpose pear with a musky flavor. It crops in early fall, bearing large pale green fruit that stores well. The tree tolerates some shade.

'Gorham' is a dessert pear with a sweet, mellow flavor. The small- to medium-sized pears have a yellow-green hue in early fall, and the skin is covered with light brown russet.

'Louise Bonne Jersey' fruits in mid-fall, producing medium-sized dessert pears with soft, juicy flesh. Its blossom is frost-resistant, but the tree still requires a sheltered site.

Pumpkin 'Jack of all Trades'

Pumpkins

Plump, glossy orange pumpkins are perhaps most famous as Hallowe'en jack-o-lanterns, but they are also delicious to eat, especially in soup or a pie. The plants are large and sprawling but, given rich soil and ample space, they are easy to grow. Sow each seed individually on its side in a pot under cover during mid-spring, or directly in the soil in early summer. Keep them well watered all summer and start feeding with tomato fertilizer every 14 days once tiny pumpkins begin to appear. For a large pumpkin, thin to one per plant; thin to 3–4 for smaller pumpkins.

Growing advice

In addition to how they are grown, pumpkin size depends on variety. For the largest, try 'Dill's Atlantic Giant'.

To prevent pumpkins from rotting as they grow, and to keep their skin clean, set developing pumpkins onto bricks or blocks to raise them off of the damp soil.

AT A GLANCE
- **Plant type** Annual
- **Aspect** Full sun
- **Soil type** Fertile and moist
- **Sow seed** Mid-spring—early summer
- **Harvest** Early fall—mid-fall

Nerine lilies

With their vibrant trumpetlike flowers, nerine lilies radiate color and bring a touch of exoticism to the garden in fall. They look delicate but are surprisingly robust and flower for several weeks. To grow well, nerine lilies need sun, shelter, and good drainage—when planted at the base of a warm wall they thrive. Nerine lilies form large, dense clumps over time and resent being disturbed, so shouldn't be lifted and divided often. In colder areas, bring pot-grown plants indoors for winter.

Which to choose

Although nerine lilies originate from South Africa, *N. bowdenii* and its varieties are fully hardy. All other species require winter protection.

N. x *bowdenii* (*right*) flowers late in the season. For earlier, and equally flamoyant color, plant daylilies (*Hemerocallis, above*) and red hot pokers (*Kniphofia*), which enjoy similar conditions.

AT A GLANCE
- ❦ **Plant type** Hardy/half hardy bulb
- ⬆ **Height** 18–24in (45–60cm)
- ◣ **Spread** 18–24in (45–60cm)
- ☀ **Aspect** Full sun
- ◎ **Soil type** Moist and well drained

Make: Instant topiary

Topiary adds real character to any garden, and can be in any size or shape you choose. Bought examples can be expensive, and starting from scratch takes years, but you can achieve a similar effect using a preshaped wire topiary frame and some ivy.

YOU WILL NEED
★ Materials:
Preshaped wire topiary frame
Suitably-sized container
Soil mix
Young ivy plants
Wire pegs
Soft string

2 Trail the stems of your ivy plants over the edge of the pot. Place the topiary frame on the container, ensuring it is vertical and positioned centrally. Push wire pegs into the soil mix to hold the frame in place.

1 Choose a pot large enough for the wire frame and for the amount of ivy you are using. Be sure the pot has drainage holes. Fill it with soil mix, then plant the ivy in evenly spaced intervals. Remove any stakes.

4 Cover the frame so that the ivy stems are evenly spaced all the way up, then pinch out their top growing tips. This will cause the plants to produce sideshoots, which you can later tie in to fill in any gaps.

5 Water the container well and place it in a sheltered position until the plants establish. Keep it well watered thereafter and tie in new stems regularly to maintain the shape. Mulch with compost in spring.

3 Take the first ivy stem and wrap it around the frame to judge how much coverage each plant gives. The stems can either be attached to the frame by tying them in place with soft garden string or by carefully weaving the stems through the wire frame.

Chusquea culeou

Bamboos

Many evergreen bamboos have attractive, colorful stems that can best be seen in fall once neighboring plants have died back. The most dramatic canes belong to tall, clump-forming bamboos, which can be planted as screens, informal hedges, or focal points. Unlike spreading or "running" types, these bamboos are not invasive—their dense clumps simply become broader over time. Once established, bamboos need little routine care, other than pruning out dead canes occasionally. To help reveal the canes, remove some of the lower leaves. Although hardy, bamboos prefer to be sheltered, away from damaging cold winds.

Controlling clumps

If space eventually becomes an issue, you can limit the size of the slowly spreading roots of the clumping bamboos, shown here. Start 12in (30cm) away from the clump, and dig an 8in (20cm) wide trench that is deeper than the roots of the bamboo. Insert a barrier made of sturdy, impermeable plastic, refill the trench, and firm the soil in well.

AT A GLANCE
- ❀ **Plant type** Hardy grass
- ⬆ **Height** 6–30ft (2–10m)
- ◣ **Spread** 6–9ft (2–3m)
- ☼ **Aspect** Full sun or partial shade
- ◉ **Soil type** Moist but well drained

Which to choose

The tall and elegant *Chusquea culeou* (*left*) forms a dense clump of attractive, glossy green canes with a banded appearance. Its foliage resembles bottlebrushes.

Yellow groove bamboo, *Phyllostachys aureosulcata* f. *aureocaulis,* is a colorful choice for the back of a border. Spent canes make handy garden stakes.

Black bamboo, *Phyllostachys nigra*, produces dark green canes that take 2–3 years to mature to glossy black. It is a good choice for Asian-style gardens.

Celery root
'Monarch'

Celery root

Related to celery and with a similar taste, this unusual vegetable is steadily acquiring gourmet status. Although it looks like a root crop, the edible part is the plump, knobbled stem from which the leaves sprout. Start the seeds under cover in early spring (*see pp.72–73*), and plant them outside in early summer 18in (45cm) apart. Cold spells can make them "bolt" (flower suddenly) so cover them with a frost blanket at first. Keep the plants well watered and don't worry if they appear to grow slowly; they put on a growth spurt in fall. Harvest celery root between mid-fall and early spring.

Growing advice

Once planted, celery root needs little routine care other than regular watering. The crop can become tough if the plants dry out in summer.

In addition to the plump main stem at the base of the plant, the leaves and fleshy leaf stalks are also edible, and have a strong celery-like flavor. Pick individual leaves sparingly to flavor soups and stews.

AT A GLANCE
- ❦ **Plant type** Hardy biennial
- ☀ **Aspect** Full sun
- ◉ **Soil type** Fertile, moist, well drained
- ⋎ **Sow seed** Early spring—late fall
- ◎ **Harvest** Late spring—winter

Brussels sprouts 'Trafalgar'

Brussels sprouts

Named after the city where they were first discovered, this essential winter crop can span the first to the last frost. In fact, frost plays a useful role in their flavor, making them taste sweeter. Brussels sprouts are easy to grow but need plenty of space, so are best for larger plots. Sow seed in early to late spring in a seedbed, before transplanting them to their final positions in late spring or early summer, 24in (60cm) apart. Cover young plants with nets to protect them against being attacked by pigeons. Brussels sprouts can become top-heavy and may topple over, so insert stakes for support, or mound up soil around the base of each stem to keep the plants upright.

Optimum growing conditions

Brussels sprouts grow best in medium to heavy soil that is well drained and has not had any manure dug into it recently; if there is too much nitrogen in the soil, the sprouts will be loose and elongated. If you prefer smaller sprouts, plant the seedlings slightly closer together than 24in (60cm) each way.

AT A GLANCE
❦ **Plant type** Hardy biennial
☼ **Aspect** Full sun
◉ **Soil type** Rich, moist, and fertile
↓ **Sow seed** Early spring—late spring
◎ **Harvest** Early fall—early spring

Growing advice

Once they are in their final growing position, keep the plants well watered. To promote a larger crop, feed in fall with a high-nitrogen fertilizer.

Harvest Brussels sprouts as required from the base of the plant upward, snapping them off downward. Surplus sprouts can be frozen.

Sprout tops, the leafy crown on top of the stem, make an excellent cabbage-like crop. Harvest it once the sprouts have been picked.

Plants for
Fall foliage

Every garden needs deciduous trees, shrubs, or climbers that develop spectacular leaf color in fall. Whether you have a large or small plot, there are a range of stunning plants to choose from.

1 *Betula alleghaniensis* Known as the yellow birch, the leaves of this tree turn rich buttery yellow.
🌳 40ft (12m) ◣ 25ft (8m)

2 *Parthenocissus tricuspidata* A fast-growing climber, Boston ivy turns bright crimson in fall. It is best for walls, and needs ample space.
🌳 40ft (12m) ◣ 25ft (8m)

3 *Liquidambar styraciflua* A great tree for fall color, its aromatic leaves pass through a riot of shades before they drop off.
🌳 80ft (25m) ◣ 40ft (12m)

4 *Amelanchier lamarckii* An all-season tree with spring blossom, summer fruit, and fall color.
🌳 4ft (1.2m) ◣ 4ft (1.2m)

5 *Prunus sargentii* A flowering spring cherry, its leaves turn bright orange and red in fall.
🌳 70ft (20m) ◣ 50ft (15m)

6 *Cornus kousa* Grown for its spring flowers, the leaves of this small tree turn crimson in fall.
🌳 22ft (7m) ◣ 15ft (5m)

7 *Rhus typhina* '**Dissecta**' The finely cut leaves of this large shrub turn vivid yellow and red.
🌳 6ft (2m) ◣ 10ft (3m)

8 *Hydrangea quercifolia* This shrub flowers in summer, and its oaklike leaves turn red in fall.
🌳 6ft (2m) ◣ 8ft (2.5m)

9 *Parrotia persica* In fall, each leaf on this handsome tree appears to be a different shade of either red, orange, yellow, or purple.
🌳 25ft (8m) ◣ 30ft (10m)

10 *Euonymus alatus* This spindle tree comes into its own during fall, when its green foliage turns dazzling crimson.
🌳 6ft (2m) ◣ 10ft (3m)

Acer palmatum 'Trompenburg'

Maples

Graceful in spring and summer, maples become an inferno of color just before their leaves drop in fall. Botanically named *Acer*, they range from cascading shrubs to stately trees, and all are easy to grow. New acers are best planted while dormant (*see p.272*), so they have time to establish a little before spring. All are fully hardy but those with small or dissected foliage can be damaged by drying winds in summer, so are best given sheltered positions. Maples don't require regular pruning but oversized trees can be cut back hard in fall or winter.

AT A GLANCE
❧ **Plant type** Hardy deciduous trees/shrubs
⚘ **Height** 8–70ft (2.5–20m)
◣ **Spread** 8–70ft (2.5–20m)
☀ **Aspect** Full sun or partial shade
◉ **Soil type** Fertile, moist, well drained

Growing advice

In addition to their vivid tints in fall, there are many acers you can grow that also provide welcome interest at other times of the year.

The spring foliage of many acers, such as *A. pseudoplatanus* 'Brilliantissimum' (*above*), is richly colored until it fades in midsummer.

From summer to fall, the intricately cut foliage of the Japanese maple, *A. palmatum*, is seen at its most beautiful and textural.

The bare, leafless stems of some acers, such as *A. pensylvanicum* 'Erythrocladum' (*above*), seem to glow in the soft light of winter.

Choosing maples

This is a large and varied group of trees and all but the Japanese maples, *Acer palmatum*, grow quickly. Most develop stunning tints in fall, although for maximum interest, consider those that also have deep bronze or brightly variegated leaves in summer. These are leafy trees and form large, dense canopies in time, so bear in mind the shade they'll cast when deciding which to grow.

Acer cappadocicum
'Aureum'

A. rubrum

A. platanoides
'Crimson Sentry'

A. negundo
'Flamingo'

A. platanoides
'Drummondii'

A. palmatum

Ideal for pots

Slow-growing Japanese maples,
A. palmatum (*right*), are the best for
containers, with both weeping and
upright forms, plus those with colored
and dissected leaves. Plant into a large
container filled with soil mix, and
position it in a sheltered spot away
from the midday sun. Water regularly
throughout summer and mulch with
garden compost during early spring.

Border trees

In addition to growing in containers,
A. palmatum and its varieties are also
ideal for planting in borders. Other
good choices include *A. negundo*
'Flamingo', which has variegated leaves
(*see left*), and *A. shirasawanum* 'Aureum',
with its bright yellow-green summer
foliage. Both then also develop fiery
tints in fall before their leaves drop.

Large gardens

Many maples can grow very large and
make excellent specimen trees in bigger
gardens. More colorful choices include
A. platanoides 'Drummondii', which
has cream-variegated foliage (see *left*),
and *A. cappadocicum* 'Aureum', which
has acid-yellow young leaves in spring
(*see far left*) that mellow during summer.
Both also develop rich tints in fall.

Cyclamen hederifolium

Hardy cyclamen

Blooming before their leaves appear, fall-flowering cyclamen, *C. hederifolium*, provides weeks of color in shades of pink or white. They are ideal for planting in rockeries or beneath deciduous shrubs, where they freely bloom below the disappearing canopy. The marbled leaves offer interest through winter and then die back in spring. Plant them while in growth and deadhead the spent blooms unless you want them to self-seed (*see below*). These bulbs need little care. Once planted, simply mulch in spring with well rotted garden compost.

Growing advice

If left undisturbed and allowed to set seed, *C. hederifolium* slowly forms attractive colonies. The plants may also naturally hybridize with each other, resulting in a carpet of flowers in varying shades of pink and white.

AT A GLANCE
- ❧ **Plant type** Hardy bulb
- ☙ **Height** 4–6in (10–15cm)
- ◣ **Spread** 6–8in (15–20cm)
- ☀ **Aspect** Dappled shade
- ◉ **Soil type** Well drained and humus-rich

Winter squashes

Squash 'Turk's Turban'

So-named because they keep well during winter, these squashes need a couple of months in storage to develop their nutty flavor. Sow seeds under cover in mid-spring to plant later, or sow directly in the soil in early summer. These large trailing plants need rich soil, so dig in garden compost before planting. Keep them well watered and feed with tomato fertilizer when the first squashes begin to swell. Harvest in late summer when they reach full size, leaving some of the stalk attached. Store them in an airy, frost-free place.

Protect from frost

Don't be fooled by the tough, robust shell of the winter squash. It is no hardier than the zucchini, its delicate-skinned relative, so never plant winter squash seedlings or young plants out in the open until all threat of frost has passed. Later, the large-leaved squash foliage will smother any weeds nearby.

AT A GLANCE
- ✿ **Plant type** Annual
- ☼ **Aspect** Full sun
- ◉ **Soil type** Fertile and moist
- ∨ **Sow seed** Mid-spring—midsummer
- ◎ **Harvest** Late summer—early fall

Which to choose

Winter squashes come in a variety of shapes, sizes, and colors. All have a firm flesh that develops a mild, nutty flavor with time.

Crown prince squashes have pale blue-gray skin and bright orange flesh. If thinned, a crown prince squash can reach 9lb (4kg) in weight.

Acorn Squashes have a green or yellow skin and orange flesh, and reach up to 8in (20cm) in length. Varieties include 'Honey Bear'.

Butternut squashes are the most widely grown and have pale orange skins with darker flesh. They can reach 10in (25cm) in length.

Leek 'Blue Solaise'

Leeks

With a sweet, mild taste reminiscent of onions, leeks are a staple crop from fall to spring, and can be left in the soil until needed. They are hungry plants, so prepare the soil the previous fall or winter by digging in well rotted garden compost. Seed can be sown under cover or outside, ready to plant starting in late spring when the seedlings are the thickness of a pencil. Keep the plants well watered in summer. Remove any weeds—leeks hate competition. Harvest baby leeks in late summer.

Growing advice

Leek stems are made sweeter by excluding light. To do this, plant seedlings deeply (see below). Soil can also be piled around adult plants.

To plant leek seedlings, trim their roots, then make narrow holes 6in (15cm) deep, spaced 8–12in (20–30cm) apart. Drop in the leeks and trickle water into the holes so they partially backfill with soil.

AT A GLANCE
- **Plant type** Hardy biennial
- **Aspect** Full sun
- **Soil type** Fertile, moist, well drained
- **Sow seed** Early spring—late spring
- **Harvest** Fall—mid-spring

Shrubs for
Fall berries

1

2

3

In addition to fiery foliage, fall is the season for decorative berries and fruits, which can provide color for many months. They are also an essential source of food for wildlife in winter, giving even more reason to grow them.

5

4

1 **Berberis thunbergii** This spiky deciduous shrub bears glossy, long-lasting fruit in fall.
🌳 3ft (1m) ◣ 8ft (2.5m)

2 **Symphoricarpos x doorenbosii** A large deciduous shrub, it has small white flowers in late summer, followed by plump white berries.
🌳 6ft (2m) ◣ 12ft (4m)

3 **Rosa rugosa** This tough shrub rose has scented summer flowers followed by glossy round red hips.
🌳 5ft (1.5m) ◣ 5ft (1.5m)

4 **Aronia x prunifolia 'Brilliant'** The white flowers of this shrub give way in fall to red and black berries, and wine-red foliage.
🌳 6ft (2m) ◣ 10ft (3m)

5 **Cornus kousa** Mature shrubs bear strawberry-like fruits in summer, which turn red in fall.
🌳 22ft (7m) ◣ 15ft (5m)

6 **Cotoneaster horizontalis** Best planted against a wall, this deciduous shrub is smothered with small red berries during fall.
🌳 3ft (1m) ◣ 5ft (1.5m)

7 **Cotoneaster salicifolius** This large arching evergreen shrub bears abundant glossy red berries.
🌳 15ft (5m) ◣ 15ft (5m)

8 **Pyracantha 'Orange Glow'** This deciduous shrub has white flowers followed by orange fruit.
🌳 10ft (3m) ◣ 10ft (3m)

9 **Euonymus europaeus** Boldly colored fall leaves accompany red fruits on this deciduous shrub.
🌳 10ft (3m) ◣ 8ft (2.5m)

10 **Callicarpa dichotoma** Known as beauty berry, this deciduous shrub has striking glossy purple fruits that persist into winter.
🌳 4ft (1.2m) ◣ 4ft (1.2m)

Jobs to do:
Fall

Around the yard:
- Renovate lawns before winter.
- Protect tender plants from frost.
- Regularly rake up fallen leaves.

In the vegetable garden:
- Harvest fruit and vegetable crops.
- Prepare the soil ready for spring as beds become empty.

In beds and borders:
- Plant new trees, shrubs, and perennials.
- Divide congested perennials.
- Plant spring-flowering bulbs.

Early Fall

This is a productive time in the garden with fruit trees and late vegetables coming into full harvest, so take time to pick, cut, or pull your maturing crops regularly. As plants die back, clear away and add any spent growth to the compost pile to help control pests and diseases for next year.

Crops to sow:

Outside: Lettuces and Swiss chard (under cloches).

Crops to plant:

Strawberries.

Harvest now:

Apples, eggplants, fall-ripening raspberries, beets, blackberries, blueberries, Brussels sprouts, calabrese, carrots, celery, cherries, chilies, zucchini, cucumbers, Florence fennel, green and string beans, kohlrabi, leeks, lettuces, maincrop potatoes, onions and shallots, pears, peas, peppers, plums, pumpkins, radishes, spinach, squashes, strawberries, summer cabbages and cauliflowers, rutabagas, corn, Swiss chard, and turnips.

Essential jobs:

* Order bare-root trees, shrubs, and fruit plants (*see p.258*).
* Plant trees and shrubs you plan to grow in containers (*see pp.258–259*).
* Lift tender bulbs and bring them under cover (*see p.259*).
* Cut back perennials as their stems die off (*see p.259*).
* Plant spring-flowering bulbs, except tulips (*see p.260*).
* Clear away spent annual bedding displays (*see p.261*).
* Divide overgrown perennials and congested bulbs (*see p.261*).
* Renovate your lawn in time for winter (*see p.262*).
* Dry chilies (*see p.263*).
* Prepare fall bedding displays and containers (*see p.263*).

Last chance to:

* Sow new lawns from seed (*see p.81*).
* Trim and tidy evergreen shrubs and hedges (*see p.83*).

Continue to:

* Prune out reverted growth on variegated plants (*see p.191*).
* Deadhead flowering plants to prolong the display.
* Water plants growing in containers during dry spells.
* Feed bedding plants growing in containers and baskets.
* Weed beds, borders, and vegetable patches.
* Add plant debris from around the yard or the beds to the compost pile.

Watch out for:

* Powdery mildew on fruit and vegetables —water well and pinch off infected leaves.

Pumpkin season

Pumpkins are ready to harvest when their skins are hard and they sound hollow when tapped. Cut the fruit off with its stalk (don't use it as a handle— it can damage the fruit) and raise the fruit off the damp soil onto blocks. Let the fruit stand in the sun for ten days to "cure" before carving or storing.

Many spring-flowering bulbs, such as crocus and daffodil, can be planted in lawns and left to naturalize over many years. Scatter the bulbs randomly and plant them where they fall. Use a bulb planter to make holes in the turf, plant the bulb at three times its depth, then replace the turf plug.

Buying bare-root trees and shrubs gives you the best choice, especially when choosing fruit varieties. Order them now locally or order mail-order nurseries for the healthiest plants. Plant them as soon as soon as you receive them following the instructions for container-grown trees and shrubs (*see p.272*).

Planting trees and shrubs in containers

1 Choose a container (make sure it has drainage holes in the bottom) that provides enough space for your tree or shrub to grow for a number of years. As a guide, use the plant's original pot to help you choose the correct size.

2 Cover the drainage holes in the bottom with pebbles so water can drain through them freely. Fill the container with soil mix, using the old pot as a guide.

Tender bulbs can be lifted and stored under cover once their top growth has died back. Brush the soil off of bulbs like begonia and gladiolius and store them wrapped in dry, airy material, such as straw. Leave dahlias until they have been frosted and their leaves blackened, then cut the stems down, lift the tubers, and store them in trays of dry soil mix.

Remove baby figs that are any larger than a pea—they won't develop any further at this time of year and will rot away. Only small figlets survive the winter, and then develop the following summer to reach maturity. To help ensure their survival, cover the figlets with a frost blanket or horticultural fleece in late fall to protect them.

Cutting back spent perennials helps keep your beds and borders tidy, and removes hiding places for pests and diseases. Leave those with attractive seedheads, however, such as sedums (*see pp.218–219*), since these will give the garden interest in winter and will provide food for birds. Don't cut back penstemons—their woody growth helps to protect them from frost.

3 Lift the old pot out carefully to prevent the soil mix from collapsing into the planting hole you have made.

4 Place the tree or shrub into the planting hole and add (or remove) soil mix until the top of the rootball sits 2in (5cm) below the rim of the container, and is level with the surrounding soil mix. Gently firm the plant in with your hands and water it thoroughly.

To harvest apples at their best, hold the fruit in your hand and gently twist. It should come away easily with its stalk. Pears should be firm and plump, and their skin may change color. They can be picked slightly underripe as they continue to ripen after picking.

Clearing away plant debris as ornamentals and vegetable crops begin to die back is an effective way to deter the build-up of pests and diseases by denying them somewhere to lurk during winter. It also keeps the yard and beds tidy. Healthy debris can be added to the compost pile but take diseased material to your local waste disposal unit.

Hardy perennial vegetables, such as asparagus, rhubarb, and globe artichokes, should be cut back at this time. Prune yellowed asparagus foliage down to ground level. Cut back old rhubarb stalks to leave the buds exposed to the cold over winter. Remove the stems of globe artichokes and cover with a thick mulch of straw or bark to protect the crown.

Spring-flowering bulbs are best bought early for the largest choice and healthiest bulbs. Plant them as soon as you can at a depth of three times the height of the bulb. If you can't plant them immediately, store bulbs somewhere that is cool, dark, and well ventilated. Plant tulips late in fall to avoid the disease known as *tulip fire* (*see p. 40*).

Growing new plants from hardwood cuttings

Cut woody stems 6–12in (15–30cm) long and remove the soft top growth, cutting above a bud at an angle. Dip the bottom into hormone rooting powder. Plant the stems two-thirds deep into containers of soil mix outdoors. They will take root and be ready to plant next fall—check for roots by pulling gently.

Summer bedding plants will be past their best and should be removed. If you haven't already saved seed from annuals, such as cornflower or marigold, it's not too late (*see p.200*). Dig up the spent plants and add them to the compost pile, along with any other undiseased plant debris.

Dividing perennials and bulbs

1 Lift the perennial or clump of bulbs from the soil with a digging fork or spade, being careful not to damage the roots. Extra-large clumps may need to be lifted in sections so they are easier to lift and handle. Shake off the excess soil so you can see the rootball clearly.

2 Divide the clump into smaller sections, each with healthy bulbs, buds, or shoots. Most bulbs, such as lily, can usually be split using your hands but established perennials may need prizing apart using two digging forks or spades held back-to-back.

3 Check each of the divisions for signs of weak or diseased growth, or dead areas, and check the roots. When you divide clumps of bulbs, such as nerine lily, discard the oldest bulbs at the center that no longer flower, and keep the young, healthy ones near the outside.

4 Replant the divided perennials and bulbs as soon as possible, at the same depth as the original clump. Prepare a planting hole, spread the roots out well, and backfill with soil. Firm the plants in and water well. Continue to water regularly as they reestablish.

Renovating your lawn

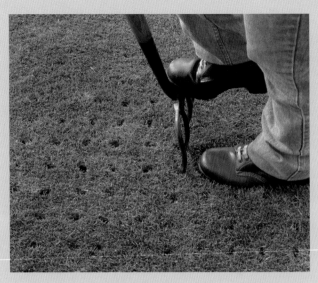

1 Grass clippings, moss, and plant debris regularly build up in lawns, which stifles growth and encourages more moss, as well as disease. Remove it each year using a steel-tine leaf rake (*above*) and add it to the compost pile. This may leave your lawn looking messy at first but it will soon recover.

2 Aerating the lawn by spiking it all over improves drainage and airflow, which encourages healthy growth and helps control moss. Using a digging fork, and wiggling it back and forth, pierce holes at 6in (15cm) intervals. Focus on areas that are heavily used or where the ground is compacted.

3 "Top dressing" is a sand and soil mixture, sold in garden centers and online, which is applied to lawns after aerating them. When spread evenly over the lawn, it improves surface drainage, which promotes lawn health and helps control moss. Apply top dressing at the rate specified on the bag.

4 Using a push broom or rake, spread the top dressing evenly over the lawn, working it into the fork holes. More can be added if necessary to even out shallow dips and small hollows to create a level surface. Water the lawn with a fine spray to help settle the top dressing, unless rain is forecast.

Winter and spring bedding plants can be planted now for colorful displays. Choose suitable containers with plenty of drainage holes and partially fill them with peat-based soil mix. Add some spring-flowering bulbs, like tulip and dwarf daffodil, cover with soil mix, then plant a mixture of bedding plants on top for a long-lasting display. Position the container in a sheltered site if possible.

Spring cabbages that were sown outside in late summer can be transplanted into their final positions now. Refer to the spacings given on the seed package and plant them accordingly. Water well and cover immediately with fine plastic nets, pulled taut, to protect against attacks by pigeons.

Maincrop potatoes are ready to lift when their leafy top growth turns yellow. Cut the growth back, wait for about ten days, then carefully dig up the potatoes using a digging fork. Let the tubers dry out on the soil for a few hours (or inside if the weather is wet). Then store them under cover in paper sacks.

Drying chilies to store them is a great way to make use of a surplus crop, and means you can use them throughout the year. Thread the fresh chillies onto string or raffia and hang them in a warm, well ventilated spot under cover until the skins are dry, dark, and crisp. Use as needed.

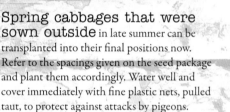

Mid-fall

Although the days are still warm, the nights will get colder, so now is the time to start protecting tender plants from frost by bringing them under cover or providing them with protection outside. Clearing fallen leaves is also an important task now, since they can smother lawns and plants.

Essential jobs:

✱ Cut and dry attractive seedheads for indoor displays (*see p.265*).
✱ Rake fallen leaves from all around the yard and the beds (*see p.266*).
✱ Plant new deciduous hedges, such as beech (*see p.266*).
✱ Leave winter habitat areas in place for garden wildlife (*see p.267*).
✱ Insulate greenhouses against frost using bubble wrap (*see p.267*).
✱ Cut back climbing roses to avoid wind damage (*see p.267*).
✱ Prepare the soil in empty beds for spring (*see p.268*).
✱ Protect tender plants outside against frost (*see p.268*).
✱ Move smaller tender plants, such as those in containers, under cover for winter (*see p.269*).

Last chance to:

✱ Lift tender bulbs before the hard frosts arrive (*see p.259*).
✱ Finish harvesting tender crops growing outside, such as tomatoes.

Continue to:

✱ Plant spring-flowering bulbs, except tulip (*see p.260*).
✱ Take hardwood cuttings from hardy shrubs (*see p.261*).
✱ Cut back perennials as they continue to die back.
✱ Remove fallen leaves and plant debris floating on ponds.
✱ Order new bare-root trees and shrubs to plant soon.
✱ Put fresh water out for birds and other garden wildlife daily.

Watch out for:

✱ Coral spot fungus on trees and shrubs—prune out all affected growth.

Crops to sow:

Under cover: Broad beans and winter lettuces.

Crops to plant:

Blackberries, currant bushes, garlic, gooseberries, raspberries, and strawberries.

Harvest now:

Apples, beets, Brussels sprouts, calabrese, carrots, celery root, celery, chilies, cucumbers, eggplants, Florence fennel, green and string beans, Jerusalem artichokes, kale, kohlrabi, leeks, lettuces, maincrop potatoes, onions and shallots, pears, peas, peppers, plums, pumpkins, radishes, raspberries, spinach, squashes, strawberries, summer cabbages and cauliflowers, rutabagas, corn, Swiss chard, tomatoes, turnips, and zucchini.

Attractive seedheads

Many plants, such as *Phlomis tuberosa* (*right*) and grasses (*see p.224–225*), have attractive seedheads. You can leave these in place in the garden for winter where they will add structure. Or, you can cut and dry some for an indoor winter display.

Clearing up fallen leaves not only keeps the yard and beds tidy but also prevents them from smothering lawns and other plants. Use fallen leaves to make leaf mold, an excellent soil improver. Store the leaves in a plastic bag for a year to slowly rot down.

Plants growing in containers can be damaged by cold, wet soil mix that is poorly drained. Raising pots off of the ground using "pot feet" (*shown right*), ensures containers drain more freely. They also keep pots raised above any puddles that may form around them. Pot feet can be purchased at garden centers or ordered online.

New deciduous hedges, such as beech and hawthorn, can be planted cheaply using bare-root plants between now and late winter. Dig a planting trench, remove any weeds, and improve the soil by adding well rotted garden compost. Space the plants 1–2ft (30–60cm) apart and water them well.

Vegetable crops grown under cover, such as tomatoes, eggplants, peppers, cucumbers, and chilies, and which have finished cropping can now be removed and the spent plants can be added to the compost pile. Ripen green tomatoes by placing them in a paper bag with a banana—the banana releases a gas that causes nearby fruits to mature. Peppers and chilies won't ripen any further but can be eaten green; immature eggplants and cucumbers are best composted.

Creating habitat areas in the yard is an effective way to attract wildlife at this time of year. Leave some areas untended, such as a log pile, an area of longer grass, or a spot under a hedge or behind the compost pile. These will be places where wildlife can find refuge from the weather or predators. If you are having a bonfire, check it for hiding animals before igniting.

Shortening tall stems on climbing roses helps prevent them and their support from being damaged by strong winds between now and winter, when they are pruned (*see p.309*). Cut back only the tall, thin stems produced this summer, plus any weaker growth.

Prepare greenhouses for winter by removing any shading material used in summer and adding any plants you don't want to keep to the compost pile. For protection against frost, line the inside with bubble wrap. This can be held in place using thumb tacks in wooden greenhouses or special clips for aluminum ones. On sunnier days, open the windows for a few hours for ventilation.

Forking the soil between plants will bring pests to the surface, where birds will find them, and will help to loosen and aerate the earth. Remove any large stones and weeds, and mulch around any slightly tender or newly planted shrubs or perennials.

Dig over the soil in empty vegetable beds and prepare it in time for spring before it becomes too wet or frozen. Dig down to a fork's depth and incorporate plenty of well rotted garden compost or farmyard manure. Remove any weeds and level the soil surface afterward.

Large tender plants that can't be brought under cover, such as bananas, ginger lilies, and tree ferns need protection from frost when left outside over winter. Wrap them completely using a frost blanket, burlap, or straw. Secure it using garden twine or chicken wire. Check after periods of bad weather to ensure the protection is still in place and resecure it if necessary.

Repotting container-grown trees, shrubs, and fruit bushes

1 If a tree or shrub has grown too large for its pot and is looking sickly, it's time to repot it. Water the plant well to loosen the soil, and ease it from the pot. You may find it helps to place the pot on its side.

Removing the yellowing leaves from Brussels sprout stems helps prevent disease. Now is also the time to support these top-heavy plants by inserting stakes or by mounding up (or "hilling") soil at the bottom of the stem.

Moving tender plants under cover is the safest way to protect them from frost. A frost-free greenhouse or porch would be ideal, but since most plants are dormant at this time, they could also be kept in a shed or garage.

Covering bare soil with black plastic is a useful way to keep it workable for spring. Any bare soil can be covered, which stops it from becoming too wet, and also controls weeds. Make sure the plastic is securely weighed down.

3 Remove any dead roots—look for any that are dry, crumbly, or show signs of mold. Also check for soil-borne pests, such as vine weevil grubs.

2 Using your fingers, carefully remove some of the outermost soil from the rootball to expose the roots. Be careful not to disturb the main part of the rootball.

4 Replant into a larger pot with good drainage. Pour soil mix into the bottom and stand the rootball on top. Fill around it with more soil mix so that the plant is at its original depth and 2in (5cm) below the rim. Water it thoroughly.

Late **fall**

As the days continue to shorten and temperatures drop, make the most of the time you can spend outside in the garden. The soil will stay warm for several weeks to come, making this a good time to choose new plants, and to plan and make changes to your planting schemes.

Essential jobs:

✱ Plant tulip bulbs (*see p.271*)

✱ Plant new bare-root ornamental and fruiting trees and shrubs (*see p.272*).

✱ Protect fruit trees from pests using grease bands (*see p.272*).

✱ Lift and divide overgrown aquatic plants (*see p.273*).

✱ Provide support for taller winter crops, such as Brussels sprouts and kale (*see p.273*).

✱ Prune fruit trees to remove cankerous growths (*see p.273*).

✱ Clean and put up bird nesting boxes (*see p.273*).

✱ Protect terra-cotta pots from frost damage using bubble wrap.

✱ Drain small decorative water features until spring.

Last chance to:

✱ Plant spring-flowering bulbs, such as daffodil (*see p.260*), and winter bedding plants (*see p.263*).

✱ Insulate greenhouses with bubble wrap (*see p.267*).

✱ Move smaller tender plants under cover before the hard frosts arrive.

Continue to:

✱ Clear fallen leaves and make leaf mold (*see p.266*).

✱ Plant new deciduous hedges, such as beech (*see p.266*).

✱ Dig and weed beds as they become empty (*see p.268*).

✱ Mulch slightly tender plants outside to protect them from frost.

✱ Compost healthy plant debris.

Crops to sow:

Under cover: Broad beans

Crops to plant:

Apples, blackberries, blueberries, cherries, currants, figs, garlic, gooseberries, pears, plums, raspberries, and rhubarb.

Harvest now:

Apples, Brussels sprouts, carrots, celery, celery root, Jerusalem artichokes, kale, kohlrabi, leeks, maincrop potatoes, parsnips, radishes, spinach, summer cabbages, rutabagas, Swiss chard, and turnips.

Watch out for:

✱ Grey mold on fruit and vegetables—remove and discard infected growth.

Tulip time

Now is the best time to plant tulips since the colder soil will mean that *tulip fire*, a disease fatal to the plants, is less likely to spread. Plant the bulbs to a depth of three times their height, spaced a couple of inches apart. Bulbs in pots can be planted more closely.

Planting bare-root trees and shrubs

1 Dig a hole wide enough for you to spread the roots out, and deep enough for the plant to be at its original depth. Pour some garden compost into the hole and then drive in a stake if planting a tree or larger shrub.

2 Set the plant in the hole and spread out its roots. To ensure it's planted at its original depth, lay a spade across the hole and position the plant so the top of the soil mark on the trunk or stem is at soil level. Add or remove soil as required.

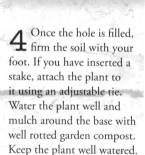

3 Make sure the tree or shrub is upright and facing the way you want. Then, fill the hole gradually using your hands to work the soil in between the roots to eliminate any air pockets. Firm the soil down at regular intervals.

4 Once the hole is filled, firm the soil with your foot. If you have inserted a stake, attach the plant to it using an adjustable tie. Water the plant well and mulch around the base with well rotted garden compost. Keep the plant well watered.

Securing grease bands around the trunks of fruit trees, including apple, pear, plum, and cherry helps prevent various wingless moths from laying their eggs, which hatch into damaging caterpillars on the tree. Use ready-prepared sticky traps, or apply grease directly to the bark, about 18in (45cm) from the base of the trunk.

Congested pond plants

should be taken out of the water and divided every few years to encourage flowering and to control their size. Lift them from the pond and use a knife, spade, or fork to split them into healthy sections before replanting.

Taller-growing winter brassicas,

including Brussels sprouts and sprouting broccoli can become top-heavy. Stake them to stop them from being blown over, especially if your vegetable patch is in an exposed area. Mulch with garden compost and, if you haven't done so already, cover them with nets to protect them from pigeons.

Mature apple and pear trees often develop

"cankers"—areas of dead, sunken bark—on their branches. These kill off growth and result in weaker harvests and are caused by a fungal disease. They must be pruned out. Cut the affected growth back to healthy tissue and discard it appropriately. Seal the cut area with wound paint, available at garden centers or online.

Cleaning and putting up bird nesting boxes

1 If you have an existing bird nesting box, take it down and clean it thoroughly to reduce the risk of pests and diseases that affect bird health. Remove any old nesting materials and scrub the box inside and out with soapy, boiling water, then let it dry.

2 When positioning new bird boxes on a tree or building, site them 6–12ft (2–4m) from the ground, facing east or north to avoid the effects of full sun and strong winds. Ensure that the entrance to the box is clear of anything that would block a bird's flight path.

Winter

Signs of Winter

Most plants are dormant at this time of the year, and the garden can look lifeless—even the leaves of evergreens can curl up in the cold. If you're shivering in winter, console yourself with the fact that hardy plants need this cold period in order to flower and fruit when the warmer weather returns.

Winter solstice

The winter solstice occurs around December 21ˢᵗ, and marks the longest night and shortest day of the year. The Northern Hemisphere is now tilted at its farthest away from the Sun, resulting in less heat and lower light levels. At noon on the winter solstice, the sun is the lowest it will be all year.

Day Length

Around the winter solstice there are fewer than eight hours of daylight per day, and fewer still the farther north you go. The passing of the solstice means that days now start to get longer, although that may not seem to be the case at first. Due to the Earth's elliptical orbit, and because actual noon and that incidated on our clocks differs by a few minutes, sunrise will still appear to be getting later for a few weeks.

Weather

Winters in the US vary by location. The south and west are warmer and mild, filled with sunshine. The rest of the country can be variable, ranging from snow and ice to mild conditions, depending on the weather fronts moving in from the Pacific and Atlantic. Frosts are regular, and even the south can experience the occasional frost.

Temperature

The average US winter temperature can be as high as 75°F (24°C) in Florida to a low of -15°F (-26°C) in Minnesota. The northern and eastern states are typically the coldest. Coastal areas are generally the mildest, benefiting from the warmer sea air. The coldest month during the winter is typically February, while December has the least sunshine.

Plant science

A long period of dormancy is essential to plants that originate from temperate areas, since they can die when forced to continue growing all year. That means winter truly is a time for plants and gardeners alike to rest.

SEEDS

Annual plants overwinter as dormant seed, and one way in which they survive this period is to produce them in abundance, so that some may endure. Seeds vary greatly from plant to plant, and have different methods of surviving winter. Some have a thick outer layer that protects them from cold, while others are tiny, and fall into cracks in the soil, where they are insulated. A common characteristic is that seeds don't contain water, which means their cells can freeze for long periods without being damaged. A cold spell is essential to many seeds, and these won't start germinating until they have experienced temperatures between 41–50°F (5–10°C) for a length of time. This is called "vernalization."

Tissues rich in starch but free of water avoid damage caused by freezing.

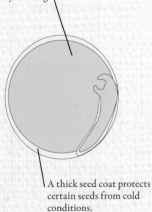

A thick seed coat protects certain seeds from cold conditions.

PERENNIALS

Most perennial plants die down completely during fall, and spend winter as dormant roots that are insulated from the coldest conditions by the surrounding soil. Their roots are further protected by containing sugars and starch, instead of water, so are resistant to cell damage caused by freezing (*see right*). Other perennials that retain visible growth above ground do so as tough, weather-resistant buds or shoots that can tolerate the cold. Instead of low temperatures, perennials are most at risk of soil that is saturated for long periods during winter. Plant roots need to breathe, which waterlogged soil prevents. Roots can effectively drown, for which most perennials have no mechanism to survive.

Sugar- and starch-rich roots resist freezing.

Insulating soil

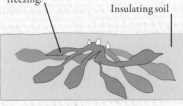

Most perennials are unable to survive in water-saturated soil.

TREES AND SHRUBS

Plants are damaged by freezing temperatures when the water in their cells freezes and expands, causing the cells to burst. This is why frozen plants turn mushy when thawed. To prevent this from happening, plants native to colder climates have evolved mechanisms to prevent their cells from freezing, or to withstand it happening. In some plants, water is pumped out of the fragile cells, leaving a sugary solution, which acts like an antifreeze that is effective to -40°F (-40°C). Some evergreens, such as rhododendron, also change the shape of their leaves, curling them to reduce their exposure to low temperatures. Most deciduous trees and shrubs protect their vulnerable dormant shoots within thick, weatherproof buds.

Water leaves the cells in plant tissues and enters the spaces around them.

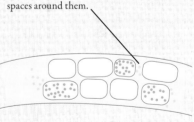

Evergreen leaves can curl inward and wilt, reducing their exposure to cold conditions.

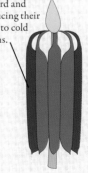

Bedding plants for
Winter color

Winter bedding plants bring a splash of color to the garden while other plants are dormant. Plant them in borders and pots in easy view from the house.

1 Polyanthus These primroses flower for several weeks in a wide range of colors if deadheaded.
🌺 4in (10cm) ◣ 4in (10cm)

2 Thyme *Thymus vulgaris* forms a colorful backdrop to flowering plants, especially variegated forms.
🌺 6in (15cm) ◣ 16in (40cm)

3 Silver Dust *Senecio cineraria* is an evergreen perennial that adds color and texture to displays.
🌺 2ft (60cm) ◣ 2ft (60cm)

4 *Ajuga reptans* An evergreen perennial, use it to provide contrast to flowering bedding plants.
🌺 4ft (1.2m) ◣ 4ft (1.2m)

5 *Bellis perennis* These double daisies bloom in shades of pink, red, and white starting in late winter.
🌺 6in (15cm) ◣ 6in (15cm)

6 Winter heathers *Erica carnea* flowers from winter to mid-spring in shades of pink or white. Some forms have golden foliage.
🌺 6in (15cm) ◣ 18in (45cm)

7 Dwarf hardy cyclamen These flower in a wide range of shades, blooming from fall to winter in all but the coldest weather.
🌺 8in (20cm) ◣ 6in (15cm)

8 Winter pansies and violas These robust plants flower continually in many shades from fall to spring. Deadhead regularly.
🌺 4in (10cm) ◣ 4in (10cm)

9 Sage *Salvia officinalis* is an evergreen shrub with green, variegated, or purple foliage.
🌺 32in (80cm) ◣ 39in (1m)

10 Winter berry *Solanum capsicastrum* is grown for its round orange berries. It is best planted in a sheltered container.
🌺 16in (40cm) ◣ 16in (40cm)

Helleborus purpurascens

Hellebores

Also known as Lenten or Christmas roses,
hellebores (*Helleborus*) flower from mid-winter
onward in endless shades of white, green, pink,
and mauve, with either plain, speckled, or
blushing faces. They thrive in shady spots, and
those with evergreen foliage offer year-round
interest. The flowers are downward-facing and
are best seen at close range, so remove last year's
foliage to appreciate them better (*see p.306*).
After they have flowered, mulch with well rotted
garden compost or leaf mold. Hellebores take
time to establish and don't like being moved or
divided. They will self-seed readily around the
garden, however, giving you ample free plants.

Partner plantings for a quiet time of year
It is easy to create an enchanting display of
delicate flowers in late winter and early spring
when the trees are bare and there is usually not
much else happening in the garden. Interplant
hellebores with crocus bulbs (*see p.37*),
snowdrops (*see pp.296–297*), or hardy cyclamens
(*see p.246–247*), and aim to achieve informal
pools and drifts of color in your planting scheme.

AT A GLANCE
- ❧ **Plant type** Hardy perennial
- ☙ **Height** 1–2ft (30–60cm)
- ☙ **Spread** 12–18in (30–45cm)
- ☀ **Aspect** Full or partial shade
- ◎ **Soil type** Fertile and moist

Which to choose

The first hellebores to flower during winter are the Christmas roses, which include *H. purpurascens* (*left*), with its beautiful green and purple-flushed flowers.

Christmas roses also include *H. niger*, which produces large white flowers in early winter. These are often flushed with pink or green, and sit above glossy evergreen foliage.

Lenten rose, *H. orientalis*, bears pink-flushed, white blooms starting from mid-winter. Its many hybrids, *H.* x *hybridus* (*above*), offer a huge range of shades and variations.

Trees and shrubs for
Winter stems

After shedding their leaves in fall, many deciduous trees and shrubs reveal colorful and textural stems and branches. Decorative bark can be slow to develop but brightly colored stems can be easily encouraged by pruning them hard in early spring (*see p.81*).

1 *Acer griseum* The paperbark maple tree has attractive coppery bark that peels naturally.
🌳 30ft (10m) 🔺 30ft (10m)

2 *Cornus sanguinea* Deciduous common dogwood, such as 'Midwinter Fire' (*see left*) has bright orange or red winter stems.
🌳 10ft (3m) 🔺 10ft (3m)

3 *Salix alba* **var.** *vitellina* **'Britzensis'** The coral bark willow is a deciduous shrub. When young its stems are red and yellow.
🌳 6ft (1.8m) 🔺 5ft (1.5m)

4 *Rubus thibetanus* This clump-forming shrub has chalky white, prickly stems. Good for borders.
🌳 8ft (2.5m) 🔺 8ft (2.5m)

5 *Corylus avellana* **'Contorta'** The twisted stems of corkscrew hazel are best appreciated in winter, and are ideal for floral arrangements.
🌳 10ft (3m) 🔺 10ft (3m)

6 *Cornus alba* Red-barked dogwood is a deciduous shrub grown for its vividly colored stems. There are many varieties to grow.
🌳 10ft (3m) 🔺 10ft (3m)

7 *Betula utilis* **var.** *jacquemontii* The brilliant white bark of the Himalayan birch tree makes a bold feature in winter, especially when the trees are planted in a group.
🌳 60ft (18m) 🔺 30ft (10m)

8 *Cornus sericea* This deciduous dogwood is grown for its stems, which can be dark red or bright lime green, such as 'Flaviramea' (*left*).
🌳 6ft (2m) 🔺 12ft (4m)

9 *Prunus serrula* The shiny chestnut-colored bark of this deciduous tree peels away as it ages, making an attractive winter feature.
🌳 30ft (10m) 🔺 30ft (10m)

Ilex aquifolium 'Bacciflava'

Hollies

The traditional image of holly may be of spiky evergreen leaves and bright red winter berries, but in reality the plant itself is far more varied. Depending on variety, many have brightly variegated foliage; some leaves are viciously spiky, while others are smooth; and some develop bright yellow berries instead of red ones. Holly, or *Ilex*, plants are male or female, and only pollinated female plants produce berries. If berries are a must, plant a male and a female holly, or choose a self-fertile variety, such as *Ilex aquifolium* 'J.C. van Tol'. Holly needs little care once established—clipping female plants to shape will result in fewer berries, however.

Versatile for landscaping

A single holly tree, or group of hollies, can be planted to provide a decorative shelter. Placed in a row, they make an effective dividing line, screen, or boundary that is also a pleasure to look at, with masses of evergreen foliage and bright berries. The best time to prune holly is summer. Watch out for aphids, which can attack young shoots.

AT A GLANCE
- ❦ **Plant type** Hardy evergreen shrub
- 🌱 **Height** 10–70ft (3–20m)
- ◣ **Spread** 12–25ft (4–8m)
- ☀ **Aspect** Full sun
- ◉ **Soil type** Moist but well drained

Which to choose

The common holly, *I. aquifolium*, is grown for its classic red berries, but for something different, try 'Bacciflava' (*left*), with its vivid yellow ones.

With variegated spiky leaves, *I. aquifolium* 'Handsworth New Silver' (*above*) is an attractive female variety. It has red berries.

Smooth-leaved hollies, such as the variegated *I.* x *altaclerensis* 'Lawsoniana' (*above*), are ideal for areas near paths or where children play.

Winter cabbages

With smooth or crinkled leaves, this leafy crop is a winter treat, especially after frost has sweetened its flavor. It needs space; 20in (50cm) between plants. It grows slowly, so is best reserved for larger plots. Sow seed under cover in spring or directly outside in summer, keep plants well watered, and feed with high-nitrogen fertilizer in late summer. Harvest the heads once they reach a usable size by cutting through the stem at soil level.

Growing advice

Sow spring cabbages in summer and grow them in the same way as winter types. Planted 12in (30cm) apart, they are more suitable for smaller plots. Harvest the heads once they reach the desired size.

Cabbage 'Savoy'

AT A GLANCE
- 🌱 **Plant type** Hardy annual
- ☀ **Aspect** Partial shade
- ◉ **Soil type** Fertile and moist
- ↓ **Sow seed** Late spring—early summer
- ◎ **Harvest** Winter—mid-spring

Evergreen shrubs for Winter interest

Evergreen shrubs provide year-round structure and color in the garden, and are especially valuable in winter when other plants have died back. Use them as hedging or in mixed borders.

1 ***Eleaganus* x *ebbingei* 'Gilt Edge'** Ideal for borders, this shrub has boldly variegated foliage.
🌱 12ft (4m) 🔲 12ft (4m)

2 ***Osmanthus heterophyllus* 'Aureomarginatus'** Known as false holly thanks to its foliage, it has fragrant white flowers in fall.
🌱 8ft (2.5m) 🔲 10ft (3m)

3 ***Fatsia japonica*** This exotic-looking plant produces large heads of white flowers in fall.
🌱 12ft (4m) 🔲 12ft (4m)

4 ***Phormium cookianum*** The slender leaves of these plants come in a wide range of colors.
🌱 6ft (2m) 🔲 10ft (3m)

5 ***Aucuba japonica*** Female plants of spotted laurel bear red berries in fall if pollinated by a male.
10ft (3m) 🔲 10ft (3m)

6 ***Hebe* 'Red Edge'** The red-edged leaves of this compact plant are attractive in winter.
🌱 18in (45cm) 🔲 24in (60cm)

7 ***Mahonia japonica*** This spiky shrub comes into its own in winter, when its striking foliage is complemented by yellow flowers.
🌱 6ft (2m) 🔲 10ft (3m)

8 ***Leucothoe fontanesiana* 'Rainbow'** This colorful shrub has an attractive arching habit, and bears white flowers during spring.
🌱 5ft (1.5m) 🔲 6ft (2m)

9 ***Euonymus fortunei* 'Emerald 'n' Gold'** This low-maintenance shrub is ideal for ground cover.
🌱 2ft (60cm) 🔲 3ft (90cm)

10 ***Picea pungens*** A dense conifer with blue needles, it looks especially good when planted alongside winter heathers.
🌱 50ft (15m) 🔲 15ft (5m)

Hamamelis mollis

Witch hazels

With distinctive yellow, orange, or red flowers borne on bare stems, and a heady, spicy scent, witch hazels (*Hamamelis*) bring true delight in winter. Many also develop colorful fall foliage, providing an additional season of interest. Witch hazels have a broad, spreading habit, so are best in larger sites. They will grow in partial shade, but flower more freely in full sun. Dig in plenty of organic matter when planting, and mulch in early spring to help conserve moisture. Established shrubs need little care but, initially, new plants should be protected from frost using a frost blanket.

Attracting wildlife in winter

Take full advantage of witch hazel's mid-winter fragrance by planting it where you will brush past it, for example, next to a path or not far from a door. Wildlife is attracted to witch hazels; birds, rabbits, and deer all enjoy its seeds. Deer will also browse on the plant. This will not harm it and can actually encourage the shrub to attain a fuller shape.

AT A GLANCE
- ❦ **Plant type** Hardy shrub
- ❦ **Height** 12–15ft (4–5m)
- ❦ **Spread** 8–15ft (2.5–5m)
- ☀ **Aspect** Full sun or partial shade
- ◉ **Soil type** Neutral to acid, moist but free draining

Which to choose

All witch hazels have scented flowers, but those of *H. mollis* (*see left*) are especially fragrant and fill the air with a peppery sweet aroma. Other species are equally worth choosing, however.

H. x *intermedia* flowers from early to mid-winter, and is often the first witch hazel to bloom. There are many varieties to consider, including copper-flowered 'Jelena' (*above*).

H. *japonica* (*above*) flowers from mid- to late winter, and is the latest-blooming witch hazel. It is less widely available than many other choices but has beautiful pale yellow flowers.

Make: A raised bed

Raised beds are ideal for growing vegetables and can be built to suit your needs. Their soil warms up quickly in spring, giving your crops a useful head start. Raised beds are ideal if you have limited space.

YOU WILL NEED
* **Materials:**
Pressure-treated lumber planks
Treated wooden posts
Soil and garden compost
* **Tools:**
Cordless screwdriver
Lump hammer
Spade or shovel

2 Place the frame in position and hammer wooden posts into the soil, one at each corner. Do not fix the frame to the posts yet—it needs to be removed so the soil around it can be leveled.

1 Decide what size bed you want and cut four planks to length to form the sides. Using a drill and screws, join the four sides to make a box, then temporarily nail scraps of timber across the corners to hold the bed frame square.

3 Remove the bed frame and even out the soil where it will sit to create a level base. Shovel any removed soil into the center of the bed. Add more soil and compost to start creating the bed.

4 Put the frame back in place, saw off the posts, and screw the frame to them. Set more planks onto the frame to reach the desired bed height. Screw all the planks to the corner posts.

5 To support larger beds, drive posts in along the sides and cut the tops off at the right height. Fill the bed with soil that has been improved with garden compost, rake the surface, then water it.

Galanthus elwesii

Snowdrops

These are among the first plants to flower in the New Year, and brave the coldest weather to bear their dainty white blooms. Botanically known as *Galanthus*, these small bulbs are best planted in groups for maximum impact, and will naturalize under deciduous trees and shrubs, and even in grass. Snowdrops are often sold "in the green"—in leaf after flowering— and should be planted in late winter (*see p.306*). Bare bulbs are available in fall, but can dry out, so are best bought early while fresh.

Which to choose

Most snowdrops, like *G. elwesii* (*see right*) and *G. nivalis* have single white flowers with green markings, although there are alternatives.

While there are various double-flowered varieties, such as *G. nivalis* f. *pleniflorus* 'Flore Pleno' , 'Lady Elphinstone' (*above*) has unusual yellow-green centers, making it a choice snowdrop.

AT A GLANCE
- ✿ **Plant type** Hardy bulb
- ⚘ **Height** 4–9in (10–22cm)
- ◁ **Spread** 2–4in (5–10cm)
- ☼ **Aspect** Partial shade
- ⊚ **Soil type** Rich, well drained, moist

Sprouting broccoli 'Rudolph'

Sprouting broccoli

Also known as purple sprouting broccoli, this crop is grown for its tender flower shoots, which appear over a long period in winter and spring. It is a large, slow-growing, productive plant, and is suitable for smaller plots. Seed is sown under cover in spring or directly outside in early summer. Space the plants 24in (60cm) apart, keep them well watered, and support them individually using stakes. The flower shoots should be harvested daily in winter and spring, which will encourage more to grow.

Growing advice

Sprouting broccoli is harvested by cutting the shoots, along with about 4in (10cm) of stem. The tender young leaves can also be picked.

AT A GLANCE
- ❦ **Plant type** Hardy annual
- ☀ **Aspect** Full sun or dappled shade
- ◉ **Soil type** Fertile and moist
- ⌄ **Sow seed** Mid-spring—early summer
- ◎ **Harvest** Winter—mid-spring

Jobs to do: Winter

Around the yard:
- Put out food and water for birds.
- Clear snowfall from paths, plants, and greenhouse and shed roofs.
- Prevent ponds from freezing.

In the vegetable garden:
- Warm vegetable patches using cloches.
- Harvest crops as they mature.

In beds and borders:
- Prune roses and other shrubs before spring arrives.
- Check tree ties and plants.
- Plant snowdrops "in the green."

Winter

With plants now dormant, take the opportunity to look around your yard and garden. Brush snow off of plants and structures to help avoid damage, and take measures to stop ponds from freezing over completely. Now is the time to review this year's harvests, and make plans for the year ahead.

Essential jobs:

✴ Prune fall-fruiting raspberries down to soil level.
✴ Prune wisterias by cutting back stems pruned in summer to two buds (*see p.197*).
✴ Make an air hole in the ice of frozen ponds (*see p.304*).
✴ Prune established apple and pear trees (*see p.305*).
✴ Feed the birds (*see p.305*).
✴ Move established shrubs while dormant (*see p.305*).
✴ Treat garden timber with wood preservative (*see p.306*).
✴ Prune deciduous trees and shrubs (*see p.306*).
✴ Prune flowering shrubs, group 2 and 3 clematis, and climbing roses (*see p.309*).

Last chance to:

✴ Winter prune gooseberries and fruiting currants (*see p.191*) and wisteria (*see p.197*).
✴ Plant bare-root trees, shrubs, and fruit bushes (*see p.272*).

Continue to:

✴ Support tall brassica crops, such as Brussels sprouts (*see p.273*).
✴ Put up new bird nesting boxes before spring (*see p.273*).
✴ Clear snow from the tops of greenhouses and cold frames.
✴ Knock heavy snowfall off of shrubs, especially evergreens.
✴ Keep access paths and driveways clear of snow and ice.

Watch out for:

✴ Wind and snow damage on trees and shrubs—prune back affected growth.

Crops to sow:

Early winter—under cover:
Broad beans

Late winter—under cover:
Broad beans, Brussels sprouts, celery, celery root, leeks, peas, and radishes.

Crops to plant:

Apples, blackberries, blueberries, cherries, currants, figs, garlic, gooseberries, pears, plums, raspberries, and rhubarb.

Harvest now:

Early winter:
Brussels sprouts, carrots, celery, celery root, Jerusalem artichokes, kale, leeks, maincrop potatoes, parsnips, rutabagas, spinach, Swiss chard, and winter cabbages.

Late winter:
Celery root, kale, leeks, parsnips, sprouting broccoli, and winter cabbages.

Plan ahead

Now that most leaves have fallen and the perennials have died back, take time to review your borders. See where there are gaps, or if plants are in the wrong place, and decide what changes you want to make. Browse through catalogs and choose new plants and crops you want to grow.

Winter crops can be harvested as needed, since most stop growing during cold periods and survive well outside. If the weather is especially wet or your soil is heavy, root crops may start to rot, so should be lifted and stored under cover. Brussels sprouts and winter cabbages benefit from cold periods, and taste sweeter after being frosted.

To prevent ponds from freezing over float a ball on the surface to help maintain a hole for air, which is vital for fish and aquatic wildlife. If the water has frozen, melt a hole in the ice by setting a saucepan filled with boiling water on the surface. Don't crack the ice by hand —the shock waves can harm fish.

Time to prune *Prune apple and pear trees now to encourage fruiting and healthy growth.*

Established apple and pear trees

need pruning every winter. First remove any crossing, weak, diseased, or damaged growth. Then, thin congested growth from the center of the tree to give it an open "goblet" shape. Reduce the length of vigorous branches by one-third to encourage fruit-bearing spurs to develop at their base. Older fruiting spurs should be thinned out if they have become congested.

Regularly feeding wild birds

and providing fresh water helps them survive the winter and brings them into your yard. To feed and attract a wide variety, put out a varied diet of large and small seeds and nuts, as well as fat balls. Hygiene is essential to avoid bird diseases. Discard uneaten food, and clean your bird tables and feeders regularly.

Check tree ties and stakes

on newly planted trees. Replace any ties that are frayed or broken, and make sure they are not too loose or too tight. Ties that are too tight will damage the trunk. If the stake is loose or broken, hammer it deeper into the ground or replace it.

Mature deciduous shrubs can be moved

while they are dormant. Dig soil from around the shrub to create as large and intact a rootball as possible. Plant it in its new position, firm the soil well with your foot, and keep it very well watered.

Cutting back the old leaves from evergreen winter-flowering hellebores (*left*) and epimediums allows the emerging blooms to be seen more easily. Wait until new shoots appear at the base of the plants, then trim all the old leaves and stems to the ground.

Garden furniture can be cleaned while it's not in use. Let it dry out completely and, if possible, store it under cover. Now that plants have died back or are dormant it is also a good time to treat timber structures in the garden, including fences and benches, with wood preservative. Choose a dry day.

Time to prune While they are dormant is a good time to tidy many deciduous trees and shrubs.

Deciduous trees and shrubs, including Japanese maples (*see pp.242–245*) and flowering dogwoods can be lightly pruned now. Remove any weak, damaged, or crossing branches, and any showing signs of disease. Cut back any excessively long growth produced last year, aiming to give the tree or shrub a balanced shape. Mulch with compost afterward.

Installing water butts to collect rainwater saves water, reducing bills, and allows you to store it where you often need it most. When installing a new water butt, raise it off the ground using a stand or some blocks so you can place a watering can under the spigot.

Neaten lawn edges

Now that overhanging plants have died back, it's a good opportunity to reshape your lawn. Use string, spray paint, or a plank of wood to mark the shape, and cut the edges with a spade or half moon turf edger. Do this after a spell of dry weather to avoid damaging your lawn.

Deciduous ornamental grasses that have attractive seedheads or develop colorful fall foliage, such as miscanthus (above), are often left standing over winter for their ornamental effect. As new growth starts to appear from the base of the plants, cut the tired old stems back to ground level.

Heavy snowfall can damage plants, especially evergreen shrubs and conifers, by weighing down their branches, causing them to snap. If snow builds up over several days, gently knock it off of your plants using a broom. Snow buildup can also damage greenhouses, sheds, and garden structures, so keep them clear as well.

Planting new snowdrops just after they have flowered, referred to as "in the green," helps them to establish well. They can be purchased this way from mail-order nurseries.

Cuttings taken last year will have rooted by now, and will be ready for planting in pots. Groups of cuttings grown together in a single pot should be eased out, carefully separated, and planted in individual pots. A cutting rooted on its own in a pot can be planted into a pot a few sizes larger.

Covering the bare soil on vegetable patches with sheets of black plastic or cloches helps to warm the soil early. This gives your crops a head start in spring by allowing you to sow seeds sooner, and encourages quicker growth. This approach is especially useful on heavy clay soils, which are slow to dry out and warm up after winter.

Time to prune Many climbers and shrubs can be pruned now to promote flowers and growth.

Climbing roses are pruned to create a framework of main branches, from which flowering shoots grow each year. Remove any old or weak branches from the main framework to the base, plus any weak new growth. Prune last year's new shoots back to healthy outward-facing buds and tie them in to the plant's support using string.

Shrubs that finished flowering in winter, including witch hazel (*Hamamelis*) and wintersweet (*Chimonanthus*) can be pruned now. Simply remove any dead, damaged, weak, or diseased stems, as well as any that cross over or are growing in the wrong direction. Mulch and feed afterward to encourage growth.

Floribunda, hybrid tea, and shrub roses are pruned by cutting back all of last year's new growth to healthy, outward-facing buds. Old, thickened stems should be cut to the base, and any weak new growth should be removed. Cut weak shoots back hard; strong ones only lightly. Overall, aim to give the shrubs an open, vaselike shape.

Summer-flowering clematis are pruned according to when they flower. Group 2 clematis that flower in early and late summer are cut back to their uppermost pairs of healthy buds, removing all other growth. Group 3 clematis varieties that flower from midsummer are cut back to buds 12in (30cm) above the ground.

Moss, algae, and soil that accumulate in the joints between paving slabs and block pavers can make the surface slippery and unsightly, so are best removed periodically. Small areas can be tackled by hand using a patio weeder (above), or with a special long-handled wire brush, available from garden centers. A pressure washer is ideal for cleaning larger areas.

Dahlias stored under cover can now be started into growth. First inspect the tubers for signs of decay or damage, and remove the affected areas. Plant the tubers individually into suitably sized pots, using all-purpose soil mix. Water them in and grow them under cover, repotting as necessary. They can then be planted outside once the risk of frost has passed.

Lawn mowers benefit from a thorough cleaning to remove any buildups of soil and dried grass from around the blades. Check that the blades are sharp and undamaged, and oil the wheels and rollers. If you have a gasoline mower, have it serviced before you resume using it.

Planting summer-flowering bulbs, such as gladiolus and lily, under cover now is a good way to give them a head start. This encourages an earlier display, and also helps to protect the vulnerable new shoots from pest damage. If the bulbs are to be planted into beds later in spring, plant them individually into deep containers of all-purpose soil mix, to a depth of three times their height. Water them in and grow them under cover until the risk of frost has passed. To plant container displays, choose a large pot with good drainage. Plant the bulbs as described above, but leave them in their container.

Winter color

As the daytime temperatures begin to increase, many bedding plants grow and flower more freely, and benefit from being fed with high-potash fertilizer. They will also require more regular deadheading to maintain their display.

Acknowledgments

Picture credits
(Key: l-left; r-right t-top; b-bottom; c-center)

The publisher would like to thank the following for their kind permission to reproduce their images:
Alamy Images: 46-47 (Yuriy Brykaylo); 50lb (Dave Marsden); 106tr (Dimitri Vervits); 165rb (Valentyn Volkov); 212lt (Eric Tormey)
Peter Anderson: 11lt (RHS Hampton Court Flower Show, designed by Matthew Childs); 245cc (RHS Chelsea Flower Show, designed by Chris Beardshaw); 285cb (RHS Chelsea Flower Show, designed by Prof Nigel Dunnett and The Landscape Agency).
Alan Buckingham: 18, 106tr, 110–111, 111tr, 149rc, 162–163, 187b, 227rt, 227rb, 272-273cb

Lucy Claxton: 164–165, 278, 300–301
Chauney Dunford: 306lt, 310lt, 311
Getty Images: 143lb
International Rose Test Garden, Portland, Oregon: 318–319 (Bruce Forster)
Brian North: 287rt, 243rc
Rough Guides: 204-205 (Tim Draper)
Juliette Wade: 50rt

Dorling Kindersley would like to thank:
Mark Winwood and his models for additional photography.

Proofreading: Constance Novis

Indexer: Jane Coulter

635 GARDENER'S

The gardener's year

SOF

R4002225389

SOUTH FULTON BRANCH
Atlanta-Fulton Public Library